s importance to the his-
ot only measured by the
he published under the
n name "No... ...tirety of his inte...

NOVALIS' "FICHTE STUDIES"

SSGS

STANFORD STUDIES IN GERMANICS AND SLAVICS

Edited by

EDGAR LOHNER, C. H. VAN SCHOONEVELD,
F. W. STROTHMANN

VOLUME VII

1970
MOUTON
THE HAGUE · PARIS

NOVALIS'
"FICHTE STUDIES"

THE FOUNDATIONS OF HIS AESTHETICS

by

GÉZA VON MOLNÁR

1970
MOUTON
THE HAGUE · PARIS

PT
2291
Z5
M6

LIBRARY OF CONGRESS CATALOG CARD NUMBER: 73-110955

Printed in The Netherlands by Mouton & Co., Printers, The Hague.

For
Kurt and Barbara

ACKNOWLEDGMENTS

I wish to express my deep gratitude to Professor Kurt Mueller-Vollmer of Stanford University for his friendship and critical guidance which supported me throughout my work.

I also wish to thank the other members of the faculty of the Department of Modern European Languages at Stanford University for their efforts on my behalf, in particular Professors E. Lohner, G. Schuelke, and F. W. Strothmann; Dr. Hans-Joachim Mähl of Hamburg for his kindness in supplying me with the results of his research before they were actually published; Professors C. R. Goedsche and Erich Heller of Northwestern University for their patience and encouragement; and both universities, Stanford as well as Northwestern, for their generous assistance.

CONTENTS

INTRODUCTION

A. THE TOPIC

Three questions, or rather one question asked three times in ever narrower terms, led to the topic which is to be discussed in these pages:

(1) What is the relationship between literature and philosophy?
(2) What impact did Fichte's philosophy have on Friedrich von Hardenberg, who is also known as the poet Novalis?
(3) What major tendencies of thought become apparent in those philosophical speculations which Novalis recorded in the years 1795 and 1796?

The extremely general nature of the first inquiry must be limited by concrete exemplification which leads directly into the second question. Obviously, there are many writers who at one time of their lives have been exposed to the study of philosophy, but rarely have the names of a poet and a philosopher been as closely associated as those of Friedrich von Hardenberg and Johann Gottlieb Fichte. The inseparable cohesion of philosophical and aesthetic interests in Novalis' intellectual endeavors prohibits a categorization which would stamp him either poet or philosopher to the exclusion of the other. Even René Wellek, when he considers "the parallelism between philosophy and poetry to be open to doubt", must acknowledge the doubtless integration between the two in Novalis' case. He does so, however, at the expense of Novalis' authenticity as a poet:

The German Romantic movement is studied mostly in the light of the philosophy developed by men like Fichte or Schelling, professional philosophers, and by writers like Friedrich Schlegel and Novalis, borderline cases whose actual artistic productions were neither of central importance nor artistically very successful.[1]

Schlegel's poetic productions were undoubtedly no literary landmarks: his *Lucinde* certainly did not come to be known for its artistic merits, and his *Alarcos* was practically laughed off the stage at Weimar. On the other hand, Novalis' *Geistliche Lieder* enjoyed an immediate and lasting acclaim not only amongst his closest circle of friends, but also in religious circles so that a number of Protestant song-books began to include them.[2] The *Hymns to the Night* (*Hymnen an die Nacht*) have without question become established as poetry of singular merit which Rudolf Haym describes as "... mit nichts zu vergleichen, was unsre klassische Poesie hervorgebracht hat, mit nichts auch, was wir bisher von der nachgoethischen, der romantischen Poesie kennengelernt haben".[3] *Heinrich von Ofterdingen,* the poet's eminently promising attempt to supersede Goethe's *Wilhelm Meister,* found such receptivity in literary circles ever since its first appearance in 1802[4] that its central symbol, the "blue flower" ("die blaue Blume"), has become synonymous with German Romanticism. Novalis, "poet of the blue flower" as Hiebel calls him,[5] is bound neither to his particular time nor even to his native country. His influence in European literature has been shown to extend to French Symbolism by Werner Vordtriede's most enlightening work *Novalis und die französischen Symbolisten.*[6] René Wellek's remark that Novalis' "artistic productions were neither of central importance nor artistically very successful" can-

---

[1]   René Wellek and Austin Warren, *Theory of Literature* (2d ed.; New York, 1956), p. 110.
[2]   Paul Kluckhohn and Richard Samuel (eds.), *Novalis Schriften* (4 vols., 2d ed.; Stuttgart, 1960—). For general references, this edition will appear as Kl² followed by volume number and page number. Specific references to the fragments which appear under the title of "Fichte Studies" in the second volume will be followed by Arabic numerals in parentheses to refer to page and lines.
[3]   *Die Romantische Schule. Ein Beitrag zur Geschichte des deutschen Geistes* (3rd ed.; Berlin, 1914), p. 392.
[4]   L. Tieck and F. Schlegel (eds.), *Novalis Schriften* (Berlin, 1802).
[5]   Friedrich Hiebel, *Novalis, der Dichter der blauen Blume* (Bern, 1950).
[6]   Stuttgart, 1963. We shall have occasion to refer to the contents of this work more explicitly in the last chapter.

not be substantiated.[7] Friedrich von Hardenberg is most definitely
a poet, and his involvement with philosophy must be viewed as the
necessary complement to his art.

Paul Kluckhohn dedicates an entire section in the introduction
to his edition of Novalis' works to Fichte's influence on the poet;
he begins with these words: "*Fichte.* Keines anderen Philosophen
Namen erscheint so häufig in Hardenbergs Briefen und Studien-
heften."[8] This obvious predominance of Fichte over any other
philosopher gives rise to the second question: What impact did
Fichte's philosophy have on Novalis?

Rudolf Haym discusses Fichte's influence on Novalis at some
length in his monumental work on German Romanticism. He defines the concept of 'Magic Idealism' not only as central to Novalis'
theory, but also as the culmination of the poet's dialogue with
Fichtean philosophy. The transition from *Wissenschaftslehre* to
'Magic Idealism' is explained as an extension of the ego's absolute
freedom from the purely ethical realm to all the ego's activities.
Haym is quick to point out that "in this entire doctrine of magic,
Novalis furnishes an objective commentary on his own poetic activity",[9] which establishes the theory of 'Magic Idealism' as the key
to Novalis' aesthetics. Wilhelm Dilthey had been the first to plead
Novalis' case after a period of neglect and misunderstanding. He
points the way to future investigations in his famed essay of 1865
which closes with these words:

Bis aber jemand sich dieser genauen wissenschaftlichen Untersuchung
unterzieht, werden wir es wenigstens für einen Gewinn halten, wenn
einer oder der andere, auf Grund dieser Darstellung, einmal zu Novalis
griffe, in der Voraussetzung dass seine Fragmente vielleicht doch nicht
so völlig willkürlich und zusammenhangslos, sein Ofterdingen nicht so
grenzenlos verschwommen seien, als es den bisherigen Kritikern Hardenbergs erschienen ist.[10]

Rudolf Haym gives full credit to the primacy of Dilthey's work[11]

---

[7] Wellek and Warren, p. 110.
[8] Kl[2], I, 10.
[9] "... dass in dieser ganzen Lehre von der Magie dem Poeten nur sein
eignes poetisches Tun objektiv geworden ist" (p. 422).
[10] *Das Erlebnis und die Dichtung* (2d ed.; Leipzig, 1907), p. 329.
[11] In the appendix to the second edition of *Das Erlebnis und die Dichtung,*

and relies on it in his own effort at interpreting Novalis.[12] There is, however, an essential difference between the two men's views.

Dilthey sees in Novalis' fragments traces of a theory of psychology (*Realpsychologie*) very much akin to the precepts of his own approach to 'humanistic and cultural sciences' (*Geisteswissenschaft*) as opposed to natural science (*Naturwissenschaft*):

Ganz deutlich ist nur die negative Erkenntnis, dass die Welt, wie wir sie nicht anders als nach Analogie unseres Ich aufzufassen vermögen, nicht aus der Vernunft, als dem Grundcharakter desselben erklärt werden könne, sondern aus einer gärenden Tiefe dieses Ich, welche, uns selber Geheimnis, in Wille, Gemüt oder Einbildungskraft mindestens ebenso primär hervorbreche. Das Problem der Welt löst sich uns demnach, soweit es überhaupt auflösbar ist, durch die Anschauung unseres eigenen Inneren. Das wunderbarste Phaenomen ist das eigene Dasein. Das grösste Geheimnis ist der Mensch sich selbst. Die Wissenschaft aber, welche es mit diesem höchsten Phaenomen zu tun hat, ist die Realpsychologie (p. 287).

Haym, on the other hand, gives prime consideration to the theory of 'Magic Idealism', and attributes to it a far more extensive importance for the entirety of Novalis' writings than Dilthey had claimed for his key concept of *Realpsychologie*.

Rudolf Haym's view, and with it the notion of Fichte's decisive influence on Hardenberg's intellectual development, prevailed to such a degree that even as late as 1929, after much more information had been made available,[13] the foremost Novalis scholar at

---

Dilthey refers to Haym's review: "Haym (Rez. der 'Nachlese' 1873, preuss. Jahrb. Jahrg. 1873) erkennt an, dass mein Aufsatz 'zuerst eine wahrhaft literaturgeschichtliche Analyse des Geistes von Novalis' gegeben habe" (p. 450).
[12] Oskar Walzel, editor of the third edition of *Die Romantische Schule*, states in the appendix, "Ausgangspunkt aller neueren Versuche, Hardenberg zu deuten, ist der auch von Haym verwertete Aufsatz von W. Dilthey" (p. 938).
[13] Both Dilthey and Haym had relied on the Tieck-Schlegel edition of Novalis' work (*Schriften* [2 vols.; Berlin, 1802, 1805, 1815, 1826, 1837]) which was supplemented by the Tieck-Bülow edition of 1846 (*Schriften* [6th ed.; Berlin]). In the meantime, six further editions had appeared of which those of Heilborn (*Schriften* [3 vol.; Berlin, 1901]) and Minor (*Schriften* [4 vols.; Jena, 1907]) were the most important, since they contained a great

the time, Paul Kluckhohn, can still consider Fichte, 'Magic Idealism', and poesy the interdependent triad which spans the distance from the beginning fragments to the artistic heights of *Heinrich von Ofterdingen:*

Was er mit Fichteschen Worten, aber nicht in Fichtes Denkrichtung, als "intellektuale Anschauung" und "produktive Einbildungskraft" bezeichnet hatte, was er "meinen magischen Idealismus" genannt hatte und doch nur als eine zu überwindende Periode hatte ansehen müssen, was er in seinem Verhältnis zur Natur in den "Lehrlingen" tastend erfühlt und zu deuten versucht hatte, es war im Grunde immer dasselbe gewesen, der Glaube an die schöpferischen Kräfte des Geistes und daran, in diesen Kräften einem "höheren Wesen" verbunden zu sein, das in der inneren Pluralität der Seele als "Ich höherer Art" zu ihm spreche. Nun, da er durch "die Spitzberge der reinen Vernunft," wie er rückschauend die Philosophie bezeichnete, hindurch war, erkannte er, dass Dichten der höchste Grad des Denkens und Empfindens sei, dass nur den Dichtern gegeben sei, was er von den Philosophen erwartet hatte, die wirklich schöpferische Kraft auf Grund des Erlebens der Einheit von Sinnen- und Geisteswelt, dass nur sie die Menschen zu dieser verlorengegangenen Einheit zurückzuführen oder vielmehr ihnen diese Einheit aufs neue zu schaffen vermögen.[14]

His opinion is still valid to this day, since it is incorporated without change in the most complete edition of Novalis' works which is presently in the process of being published.[15]

The continuity from Haym to Kluckhohn is by no means uniform.

---

deal of hitherto unpublished material. In 1929, Paul Kluckhohn together with Richard Samuel edited the most complete collection of Novalis' works (*Schriften* [4 vols.; Leipzig, 1929]; henceforth, this edition will appear as Kl[1] followed by volume number and page number). It remained the definitive edition for thirty-one years.

[14] Kl[1], I, 78.

[15] Since Paul Kluckhohn had died in 1957, Richard Samuel reemployed his coeditor's introduction to the first edition and made whatever changes had become necessary: "Paul Kluckhohns Haupteinleitung (Friedrich von Hardenbergs Entwicklung und Dichtung, S. 1-67) konnte vom Verfasser selbst nicht mehr durchgearbeitet werden. Sie erscheint hier in ihrer ursprünglichen Gestalt mit dem einen Unterschied, dass überall dort, wo die Forschung der letzten Jahrzehnte neue Fakten ans Licht gebracht hat, der Unterzeichnete diese eingefügt oder den Text entsprechend ergänzt hat" (Kl[2], I, vi-viii).

Even though evaluations as summarily hostile as Goedecke's[16] were on the wane, the scope of variance among those who sought to do Novalis justice widened in proportion to the increase in their number. Both Dilthey and Haym had put considerable stress on Novalis the thinker in order to explain Novalis the poet. Not only did their approach prove to be so suitable that it came to be standard, but it also focused an increasing amount of attention on those of the poet's preoccupations which were not necessarily of a literary nature. Many were the efforts at determining Novalis' identity as a thinker; the best known are the works of: Egon Fridell,[17] first to attempt a general evaluation of Novalis' philosophical significance; Heinrich Simon[18] who attaches an all-inclusive range of applicability to the concept of 'Magic Idealism' which far transcends its limitation to the realm of art as designated by Rudolf Haym; Anni Carlsson[19] who, in her attempt to shed light on Novalis' speculative background, furnishes an overall representation of the thoughts expressed in the fragments which she examines according to their topical relation; Hugo Kuhn[20] who outlines Novalis' intellectual position as one which mediates the contrast between the Kantian concept of a 'thing in itself' (it-object) and the Fichtean concept of an 'absolute ego' (I-object) by arriving at the synthetizing conceptualization of a 'thou-object'; and Theodor Haering[21] whose extensive tome assembles the entire content of Novalis' fragmentary speculations from an Hegelian point of view.

A most promising avenue of investigation was furnished by another facet of the poet's life — his religiosity, to which his family-background, the pronouncements of contemporaries, and his own writings bear sufficient witness. For instance, the disclosures offered by Sophie von Hardenberg, who hides her true identity under the

---

[16] *Grundriss* (2d ed.; Leipzig, 1898), Vol. VI, Bk. 7, Sect. 1, p. 49.
[17] *Novalis als Philosoph* (München, 1904).
[18] *Der magische Idealismus. Studien zur Philosophie des Novalis* (Heidelberg, 1906).
[19] *Die Fragmente des Novalis* (Basel, 1939).
[20] "Poetische Synthesis", *Zeitschrift für philosophische Forschung* (Meisenheim, 1951). Central to the author's argument is fragment 532 of Kl[1], III which includes the telling substitution: "Statt Nicht-Ich - Du."
[21] *Novalis als Philosoph* (Stuttgart, 1954).

modestly assumed title of a "member of the family",[22] are inspired
to no small degree by her desire to affirm her ancestor's image as
that of a devoutly religious man whose path happened to be less
orthodox than his father's.[23]

In a similar vein, A. Schubart explains in the introduction to his
monograph[24] that his hero's sure religious footing, despite an oc-
casional step in the 'wrong' direction towards Rome, sets him off
most advantageously against the dissolute contemporary background relevant to which the author refers to the brothers Schlegel
with very special ire. More penetrating analyses of the poet's
thoughts on the divine and its relation to man are contained in
Helene Overbeck's astute dissertation[25] and Karl Barth's chapter
on Novalis in his summation of protestant theology before and after
Schleiermacher.[26] Both authors are convinced that the theme of
simultaneous dualism based on the conceptualization of ego and
non-ego as two perfectly equivalent spheres is central to Novalis'
idea of the divine which must be viewed as the guarantor of that
equivalence. Overbeck proclaims Novalis a mystic insofar as the
true or absolute ego is, for him, identical with God; Barth, as so
many theologians when confronted with the phenomenon of mysticism, doubts whether Novalis has not confused the lines which
separate the empirical from the Absolute, the human from the
divine. The mystical element in Hardenberg's poetry and thought
appealed to kindred spirits from Maeterlinck[27] to Rudolf Steiner,[28]
but the most useful contributions to scholarship were made by Walter Feilchenfeld's study which traces the direct and indirect relation

---

[22] *Friedrich von Hardenberg. Eine Nachlese aus den Quellen des Familienarchivs* (Gotha, 1873).
[23] She concludes on the note that Novalis' 'Geistliche Lieder' and their
popularity in religious circles constitute the foundation of his fame. c.f.:
pp. 250-51.
[24] *Novalis' Leben, Dichten und Denken* (Gütersloh, 1887).
[25] "Die religiöse Weltanschauung des Novalis" (Berlin, 1928).
[26] *Die protestantische Theologie im 19. Jahrhundert. Ihre Vorgeschichte
und ihre Geschichte* (Zürich, 1947). The volume contains a collection of
lectures which were originally delivered at Münster and Bonn in the years
1932-33.
[27] *On Emerson and Other Essays* (New York, 1916).
[28] The title of one of his works is: *Novalis als Verkünder des spirituell zu
efassenden Christentums* (Dornach, 1930). Also, Powell Spring's *Novalis,
Pioneer of the Spirit* belongs to the school of Rudolph Steiner.

of Jacob Böhme's mysticism to Novalis's spiritual development[29] and Hans-Joachim Mähl's revealing findings concerning Novalis' study of Plotinus, or rather his study of Tiedemann's *Geist der spekulativen Philosophie.*[30]

Hardenberg's profession and his related interest in the sciences has also given rise to a number of investigations. One of Richard Samuel's many contributions to Novalis-scholarship, as well as one of Gerhard Schulz', is dedicated to his professional career[31]; W. Ohlshausen explores his scientific interests[32]; Käte Hamburger uncovers the philosophical implications in his preoccupation with mathematics[33]; and Martin Dyck also makes his mathematical studies the object of investigation by relating them to the source-material available at the time.[34]

Aside from specified investigations, Novalis is, as a matter of course, also the subject of monographs, such as Heilborn's,[35] Hederer's,[36] and Hiebel's,[37] and he occupies a place of some prominence in standard works of a more general nature, as for instance Ricarda Huch's *Blütezeit der Romantik,*[38] Nicolai Hartmann's *Die Philosophie des deutschen Idealismus,*[39] or H. A. Korff's *Geist der Goethezeit.*[40]

---

[29] *Der Einflusz Jacob Böhmes auf Novalis* (Berlin, 1922).
[30] "Novalis und Plotin", *Jahrbuch des Freien Deutschen Hochstifts* (Tübingen, 1963), pp. 139-250. The author is critical of Feilchenfeld's approach (p. 141) and of "the legend of Jacob Böhme's influence" (pp. 142-143), but Walter Feilchenfeld's conclusions cannot be invalidated in their entirety, nor can his effort as such be slighted.
[31] Richard Samuel, "Der berufliche Werdegang Friedrich von Hardenbergs", *Romantik-Forschungen* (Halle, 1929), pp. 85-112. Gerhard Schulz, "Die Berufslaufbahn Friedrich von Hardenbergs (Novalis)", *Jahrbuch der Deutschen Schillergesellschaft,* VIII (Stuttgart, 1963).
[32] "Friedrich von Hardenbergs Beziehungen zur Naturwissenschaft seiner Zeit" (Diss. Leipzig, 1905).
[33] "Novalis und die Mathematik", *Romantik-Forschungen* (Halle, 1929), pp. 113-184.
[34] *Novalis and Mathematics* (Chapel Hill, 1960).
[35] *Novalis der Romantiker* (Berlin, 1901).
[36] *Novalis* (Wien, 1949).
[37] *Novalis.*
[38] 5th ed.; Leipzig, 1913. Original date of publication: 1899.
[39] 2d ed.; Berlin, 1960. Original date of publication: 1923.
[40] 3rd ed.; Leipzig, 1958-1960. Original date of publication of Vol. III: 1940.

This representative selection of the diverse approaches available to Friedrich von Hardenberg's interpreters could easily be refined and expanded to any desired degree. It suffices, however, to establish the scope of variance in mere outline rather than in its entirety, since the purpose at hand is simply to point out that despite diversification and lack of uniformity the scholarly tradition from Haym to the present agrees in recognizing the initial importance of Fichte's philosophy to Novalis. The range of opinions may extend from those which minimize Fichte's influence on Novalis in favor of the latter's intellectual independence[41] to those which claim: "in der Fichteschen Methode und Denkform ist er Zeit seines kurzen Lebens ganz und gar befangen geblieben".[42] No matter what the individual interpretation may be, the fact remains that Novalis was undeniably preoccupied by the doctrine of the *Wissenschaftslehre* and that he came to formulate his very personal concept of 'Magic Idealism', the appropriate theoretical parallel to the merging of art and philosophy which was to become so characteristic of his poetic practice. The more specific question, however, as to how Novalis came to develop his own point of view from his early philosophical studies has never been answered, because these very studies, or rather their first recorded results, have never been the object of an independent investigation.

This neglect was initially occasioned by the editorial policies of Schlegel, Tieck,[43] and Bülow.[44] The fragments they had selected for publication from Novalis' literary estate are arranged according

---

[41]   Theodor Haering, *Novalis als Philosoph.*
[42]   E. Heilborn, p. 84. c.f. also H. Kuhn, p. 163: "Und die Wissenschafts-lehre bleibt für Novalis durchaus, bis zum Ende, bestimmend, auch als er später glaubt, ihre Anwendung weit über Fichte hinaus ausdehnen zu müssen."
[43]   We are using the second edition of 1805.
[44]   Bülow introduces no separate headings for his additional selection of over six hundred fragments, but he does mention on page x of his introduction that he follows the topological principle of his predecessors: "In sofern es seine Übelstände gehabt hätte, sie, ihren Inhalte nach, in mehrere Abtheilungen zu bringen, habe ich vorgezogen, die, Poesie und Kunst insbesondere betreffenden voranzustellen und die in Wissenschaft und Leben einschlagenden so wie sie in Novalis eignen Papieren zerstreut waren, folgen zu lassen."

to three topics: 'philosophy and physics' ('Philosophie und Physik'), 'aesthetics and literature' ('Aesthetik und Literatur'), and 'views on ethics' ('Moralische Ansichten'). Ernst Heilborn's edition of 1901 did not only include much of the material which had previously remained unpublished, but it was also an attempt to present Novalis' work in chronological order. His methods of determining this order were questioned immediately by renowned scholars like Oskar Walzel[45] and Jakob Minor,[46] so that in 1907[47] the chronological approach was again supplanted by the original topological one.

Eduard Havenstein[48] continues in the tradition of Ernst Heilborn, but he reexamines the manuscripts at Oberwiederstedt with a far more critical attitude than his predecessor. His new chronological order for Novalis' fragments is largely based on the observation that the appearance of the letters "st" undergoes a periodic change during the course of the poet's life. Havenstein's work laid the foundation to all future efforts at reconstructing the natural sequence in Novalis' writings, and Paul Kluckhohn does not hesitate to acknowledge this debt in the preface to his edition in 1929. With this edition the phase of modern Novalis scholarship begins. Not only did Kluckhohn render an improved chronological arrangement, but he also published a great quantity of new material. The earliest group of fragments which he places in the years 1795 and 1796 was particularly affected by this increase, so that a coherent investigation of the beginning stages in Novalis' intellectual development is only a comparatively recent possibility. That Paul Kluckhohn had had definite intentions of sponsoring such an investigation with his new edition is easily discernible from these words in his well-known general introduction: "Hardenbergs philosophische Studien von 1795/96, wie sie unsere Ausgabe grösstenteils zum ersten Male veröffentlicht, ... erfordern noch eingehende Untersuchungen, die das Verhältnis zu Fichte und zu Kant im einzelnen

---

45 *Euphorion*, IX, p. 456 ff.
46 *Anzeiger für deutsches Altertum*, XXVIII, p. 82 ff.
47 Minor, *Novalis Schriften.*
48 *Friedrich von Hardenbergs ästhetische Anschauungen. Verbunden mit einer Chronologie seiner Fragmente.* "Palaestra", LXXXIV (Berlin, 1909).

zu verfolgen hätten . . ."[49] Three decades later, "despite Theodor Haering's important work", Richard Samuel still finds himself compelled to allow this demand to stand unchallenged and unchanged.[50]

Novalis als Philosoph, by Theodor Haering, is singled out not only because it is the most extensive discussion of Novalis' theoretical writings, but rather because the author in his efforts to offer a comprehensive interpretation relies heavily on those very fragments mentioned by Kluckhohn. He does not treat them separately, however, since he does not deviate from the traditional method of approaching the entire body of fragments on a topological basis. In this instance, it was done with justification, because Theodor Haering argues in favor of 1797 as the recording date for the first fragments[51] which would greatly diminish their independent value as indicators of the initial stages in Novalis' development. In 1965, the new Novalis edition's second volume, which contains the fragments in question, was published under the coeditorship of Hans-Joachim Mähl whose detailed research maintains the previously assumed date of 1795/96 to be the correct one.[52] This very same

---

[49] Kl¹, I, 20.

[50] Kl², I, 11.

[51] ". . . dass die bisherige Trennung der Nachlassteile keineswegs in dem seither angenommenen Masse notwendig ist, sondern dass die uns erhaltenen Meditationen in der Hauptsache zeitlich wohl überhaupt nich so weit auseinanderliegen, d.h. durchweg mehr aus der späteren Zeit von 1797 an stammen dürften. Das angeblich 'Spätere' wird sich somit auch da, wo es, wie angedeutet, bisher eine grössere Dominanz gewisser anderer Themen als das Frühere aufzuweisen schien, noch mehr als bisher nur als eine *Ergänzung* des 'Früheren,' keinesfalls als ein Gegensatz dazu erweisen; ja, es wird sich vielfach sogar das bisher 'Frühere' als mit 'Späteren' fast gleichzeitig herausstellen" (p. 589).

[52] "Die Herausgeber konnten sich der chronologischen Auffassung Haerings nicht anschliessen, abgesehen davon, dass seine Beweisführung eine Reihe von Unklarheiten und Widersprüchen enthält. Die Bedeutung der von ihm aufgeworfenen Datierungsfrage geht aus der für die Novalis-Forschung gravierenden Frage hervor, ob die Studien *vor* oder *nach* dem Tode der Sophie von Kühn, diesem für Novalis bestimmenden Erlebnis, niedergeschrieben wurden" (Kl², II, 30). And later: "So ergibt sich also aus einer genaueren Prüfung der biographischen Zeugnisse, dass die *Fichte-Studien,* wie von Paul Kluckhohn angenommen, in die Jahre 1795/96 fallen. Erhärtet und erwiesen wird diese Schlussfolgerung allerdings erst durch eine nochmalige Beobachtung aller handschriftlichen Kriterien, die neben der bisher behandelten Datierungsfrage zugleich die *innere Chronologie* der Studien klarlegen können" (p. 37).

research[53] also produced a superior interfragmentary chronological arrangement, so that early fragments are presented in a far more coherent fashion than ever before. The editor entitles the initial fragments, those written by Novalis during the years 1795 and 1796, "Fichte Studies" (*Fichte-Studien*) because they constitute a very independent interpretation of Fichtean philosophy (". . . Konvolute, die sich in einer sehr selbständigen Auseinandersetzung mit der Philosophie Fichtes beschäftigen, . . ." Kl2, II, 30). Thus the results of most recent scholarship have made it evident once more that any personal variations contributed by Novalis to Fichtean doctrine would become apparent in a separate investigation of the first group of fragments. The feasibility of such an investigation has been increased greatly by the present edition of Novalis' works which causes the editor to finish his introduction to the "Fichte Studies" in these words: "Gerade weil diese Aufzeichnungen die Anverwandlung der Fichteschen Philosophie in ihren einzelnen Stadien bis zur Selbstfindung des Autors sichtbar machen, haben sie ihren Eigenwert und verdienen für sich allein betrachtet zu werden, was bisher noch nicht geschehen ist, da alle Darstellungen von Hardenbergs Philosophie die Studien mit den späteren Fragmenten vermischen" (Kl2, II, 102-103).

The chapters which follow were written in the hope that they may serve as a first step toward complying with a wish so persistently voiced throughout the past years. Accordingly, the field of investigations has essentially been restricted to the two primary sources: to the "Fichte Studies" and to Fichte's *Wissenschaftslehre*.[54]

---

[53] A detailed report of Hans-Joachim Mähl's editing technique is to be found in his introduction (pp. 29-103) which also includes a table of cross-references (pp. 88-89) for the order of the fragments in the edition of 1929 as compared to the new arrangement. He was kind enough to send the galley proofs of this introduction to me as early as 1963 which enabled me to make use of his findings before their actual publication. I am deeply grateful for this generosity on his part and for the words of encouragement which accompanied it.

[54] I. H. Fichte (ed.), *Johann Gottlieb Fichte. Sämmtliche Werke* (11 vols.; Berlin, 1845-1846). All references to J. G. Fichte's works apply to this edition which his son prepared, and will appear as *SW* followed by volume and page number.

B. TREATMENT OF THE TOPIC

The "Fichte Studies" present a manifold array of intellectual flashes
which kindle fires of varying duration and intensity. A particular
fragment may be a mere isolated instance, or it may initiate a chain
of speculations linked by a central topic. There is, however, no
single topic which can be said to dominate the "Fichte Studies" in
their entirety, and the unity which an interpretive attempt of any
coherence would require as prerequisite must be looked for else-
where.

Several scholars have thought the dialectic oscillations between
polar extremes to be the most characteristic feature of Novalis'
writings in general, and they have made use of it in deciphering his
intentions and thoughts which otherwise proved almost inaccessible
because of their fragmentary exposition. Karl Barth's essay on
Novalis, for instance, examines some of the most pertinent empirical dichotomies found in Novalis' fragments in order to question
their author's position with respect to the ultimate or theological
dichotomy, the relationship between man and God. The excellent
dissertations by Tscheng-Dsche Feng, "Die Analogie von Natur
und Geist als Stilprinzip in Novalis' Dichtung",[55] and by Jury
Striedter, "Die Fragmente des Novalis als 'Präfigurationen' seiner
Dichtung",[56] may serve as further examples of the same approach.
Both consider Novalis' dialectical attitude in matters philosophical
to be equally significant in determining his style. Feng declares his
intentions in these words: "In der vorliegenden Arbeit versuchen
wir zu erforschen wie ihm [Novalis] Subjekt und Objekt, Innen-
und Aussenwelt, Geist und Natur ineinanderfliessen und wie von
hier aus sein richterischer Stil entsteht" (p. 6); Striedter's approach
reflects his greater emphasis on philosophical depth: "Seit die Spal-
tung von Subjekt und Objekt in den Mittelpunkt der philosophischen Betrachtung gerückt ist, führt das Denken mit innerer
Notwendigkeit immer wieder zur Form des Gegensatzes und der
Dialektik, selbst dort wo es sich — wie beim Beispiel des Antino-
mien-Streites — nicht direkt um einen Dialog und ein Gespräch
handelt. Für das dialektische Denken ist die Form des Dialogs nicht

[55] Heidelberg, 1935.
[56] Heidelberg, 1953.

mehr Kostüm, wie bei Hemsterhuis, sondern ist darstellerische Entsprechung des Denkens selbst" (p. 20).

Although no single topic is central to the entire body of the "Fichte Studies", the manner in which Novalis treats each of the major topics follows a definite pattern. He invariably chooses a basic dichotomy as worthy of being examined at some length. For this reason, the "Fichte Studies" are dominated by juxtapositions like 'feeling - reflection' (*Gefühl - Reflexion*), 'content - form' (*Stoff - Form*), 'truth - appearance' (*Wahrheit - Schein*), 'matter - spirit' (*Materie - Geist*), 'sense perception - thought perception' (*Anschauung - Vorstellung*), 'analysis - synthesis' (*Analyse - Synthese*), and many others. All these dichotomies are ultimately nothing but variations on the most basic dualism experienced by man — the constant confrontation of subject and object, of ego and non-ego. The latter terminology has been made familiar by Fichte's *Wissenschaftslehre* where, from the very beginning, its three basic axioms (*Grundsätze*) deal with that very prime dualism and its resolution. Novalis' inspiration for his exercises in dialectics stems directly from the method followed in the *Wissenschaftslehre*. His speculations concerning the various dichotomies found in the 'Fichte Studies" are reapplications and reinvestigations of the mysterious paradox that otherness is sameness, that ego and non-ego are related. Again and again his source becomes apparent: the sentence of identity, the formula $A = A$ which stands at the beginning of the *Wissenschaftslehre*, continues to appear throughout the "Fichte Studies" either directly or implied.[57]

An exposition of the schema of interrelation between subject and object as it is envisioned by Novalis would best disclose that which is of uniform importance to the entire "Fichte Studies". The first chapter, therefore, furnishes an outline of the general schema of interrelation in its particular application to the dichotomy of subject and object. The schema which emerges is an undeniable descendant of the one Fichte has patterned in his first basic axiom (*Grundsatz*)

---

[57] This tendency has already been noticed by Kluckhohn: "Hardenbergs *philosophische Studien* von 1795/97, wie sie unsere erste Ausgabe grösstenteils zum ersten Male veröffentlichte, gehen in immer erneuten Ansätzen von dem Kernsatz der 'Wissenschaftslehre': 'Ich bin ich' und der 'Urhandlung', dem Sichselbstsetzen des 'Ichs', aus" (Kl², I, 11).

to the *Wissenschaftslehre*. There Fichte states in effect that the ego is the point at which the objective[58] and the subjective[59] realms are equated,[60] which presupposes that the ego must itself be both object as well as subject.[61] This simultaneity, in turn, is founded on the prerequisite of the ego's identity with undifferentiated being[62] or rather with the pure enactment of being.[63] The rest of the *Wissenschaftslehre* is a systematic commentary on the manifold implications contained within the first basic axiom and its two corollaries of negation[64] and limitation.[65] Much of the "Fichte Studies" is written in that spirit of the Fichtean original, that is to say, it is written as a commentary on that very axiom to which, as has already been stated, Novalis refers so frequently. Novalis' schema of interrelation also defines the ego as the point at which subjectivity and objectivity merge, and he too requires an absolute ego, an ego which is pure

---

[58-62] The Fichtean version of the sentence of identity is: "If A is posited within the ego, then it is posited; or rather — then it is." ("Wenn A *im Ich* gesetzt ist, so *ist es gesetzt;* oder — so ist es" (*SW*, I, 94). The conditional part of the sentence of identity refers to the realm which is customarily called objective experience. The unconditional part of the sentence of identity refers to the realm which is customarily called subjective experience or reflection. The fact that there is a necessary connection between the 'if' and the 'then' in Fichte's interpretation of the sentence of identity is called 'X', a relationship whose necessity is entirely due to the ego's identity with its own self as positing agent and as reflecting agent. The ego's identity is expressed by the formula I = I (*'Ich = Ich'*), which constitutes the only unconditional version of the sentence of identity. The subjective realm and the objective realm, the reflecting ego and the positing ego, are declared one insofar as they are ego, and if being may be attributed to either realm it must first be attributed to the ego per se.

The formula which outlines Fichte's argument to this point is: $(A = A) =$ (*if* A is posited, *then* A is) $= X = (I = I) =$ I am. The footnotes apply to this formula in the following order:

[58] *If* A is posited, . . .
[59] *then* A is.
[60] X
[61] I = I
[62] I am

[63] ". . . das Ich *ist,* und es *setzt* sein Seyn vermöge seines blossen Seyns. — Es ist zugleich das Handelnde, und das Product der Handlung; das Thätige, und das, was durch die Thätigkeit hervorgebracht wird; Handlung und That sind Eins und ebendasselbe" (*SW*, I, 96).

[64] The second axiom dependent on the first according to content ("Zweiter, seinem Gehalte nach bedingter Grundsatz").

[65] The third axiom dependent on the first and the second according to form ("Dritter, seiner Form nach bedingter Grundsatz").

enactment of being, in order to furnish the unity necessary to the ego's empirical function. There is, however, a telling difference between Fichte and Novalis in their respective approach to the absolute ego. Fichte admits that his absolute ego constitutes a negative value,[66] yet he goes on to explore it with the power of reason, because his primary interest lies in establishing the Absolute as heritage of the empirical ego so that it may be morally free. Novalis has no such preconceived goal and examines the empirical ego as the paradox it is, as point of tangency which both marks the dualism of subject and object and unites it. He does not stress the empirical ego's unifying aspect to the exclusion of the other, as Fichte must do in order to gain direct access to the Absolute. Quite the contrary, Novalis takes the indirect path, the *via negativa,* to the Absolute, and this constitutes his main divergence from the approach followed in the *Wissenschaftslehre.* The second chapter begins, therefore, with an exposition of Novalis' hesitancy to deal directly with conceptualizations of absolute values, and his tendency to view concepts like the 'absolute ego' as a regulative function, very much like the one Kant ascribes to 'ideas'.[67] The trend of the discussion at that point is dominated by the following two fragments:

Ich bedeutet jenes negativ zu erkennende Absolute was nach aller Abstraction übrig bleibt — Was nur durch Handeln erkannt werden kann und was sich durch ewigen Mangel realisirt (270, 28-30).

Ich — ist vielleicht, wie alle Vernunftideen blos regulativen, classificirenden Gebrauchs — Gar nicht in Beziehung zur Realität (258, 18-19).

Next, the various aspects of the concept of regulative function must be explored. In order to make it easier to follow the actual text, a brief outline of the trend of the argument will be furnished here.

A regulative function is a unifying function, and it implies that there is something to be unified, that is to say, that something is not one, but that it is rather in a state of dualism or multiplicity. The Absolute is, per definition, one; multiplicity is its negation. Nega-

---

[66] C.f. chap. ii.
[67] Ernst Cassirer (ed.), *Immanuel Kant's Werke, Kritik der reinen Vernunft,* Vol. III (Berlin, 1922), p. 244 ff.; Dr. Rudolph Eisler, *Kant-Lexikon* (2d ed.; Hildesheim, 1961), c.f. *"Idee,* transzendentale", pp. 257-264.

tion cannot stand by itself, it cannot be absolute: it has to negate SOMETHING.[68] Negation expresses, therefore, a relationship to that which it negates. The negation of unity means unity in terms of its opposite, multiplicity, or rather multiplicity in terms of unity. This related multiplicity is the realm of the empirical per se. In its negative aspect, it consists of the basic dualism between the subjective and the objective realms; in its dependency on the Absolute it consists of the basic unity, i.e., relationship, between those two realms. The empirical realm is a related dualism, a paradox which signifies ultimately that duplicity and unity are one. For Fichte duplicity and unity are one in the concept of limitation which he discusses as his third basic axiom.[69] Novalis interprets this very same notion of limit not only as the common point at which two opposing stresses meet, but also, in its inverted sense, as the common point of origin for two forces directly opposed to one another. The common point is the empirical ego as unity. Unity, however, has two aspects: it appears as whole and it appears as part. The empirical ego is simultaneously both whole and part which means that the empirical ego serves as the common point of origin for an analysis and a synthesis respectively. The analytical aspect is also commonly referred to as 'inner world' (Novalis' *innere Welt*), and the ego functions as the sphere which encloses it. The synthesizing aspect must then be understood as the 'outer world' (Novalis' *äussere Welt*), where the ego functions as the starting point for an unlimited extension into the objective realm, into the realm of the non-ego. The inner world and the outer world, the analysis and the synthesis, are opposites, yet they are also the same by reason of the empirical ego's functioning as their common point of origin. The unity of the empirical ego serves as the equating factor for the objective and subjective realms, so that one constitutes a perfect image of the other. The resultant mutually representative relationship can also be expressed by the formula $A = A$, if that equation is employed in the exact sense in which Fichte uses it. That $A = A$, or rather

---

[68] Fichte defines negation in his second axiom as: "dependent according to content" ("seinem Gehalte nach bedingter Grundsatz"), *SW*, I, 101.
[69] The third basic axiom of the *Wissenschaftslehre* ("Dritter, seiner Form nach bedingter Grundsatz"), *SW*, I, 105-110.

that the relative synthesis of the outer world is at all times equal to the relative analysis of the inner world, is due to the absolute synthesis which is also called absolute ego. The fact that the inner and the outer worlds are different from one another despite their equality is due to the absolute analysis which is the absolute ego's binary manifestation, its simultaneous subject-object directedness in the empirical realm.

We have arrived again at the very point from which we started, and the task of outlining Novalis' basic schema of interrelation has thus been completed. It has become evident that it can be summarized in terms of the Fichtean alignment of formulas derived from the sentence of identity: $(A = A) = X = (I = I) = I$ am, where $A = A$ stands for the equality of the subjective and objective realms, X for the equating factor prerequisite to such a relationship, $I = I$ for the fact that it is the ego which constitutes the equating factor as which it must necessarily partake of the dualism it unites, and "I am" for the absolute unity of the ego's being, for the ego as *actus purus* or *Tathandlung,* from which its empirical power of unification is derived directly and its dualistic empirical state indirectly. This schema of interrelation is basic to the "Fichte Studies", and of the many formulations in which it appears, the following quotation is cited in the second chapter as the most appropriate summary statement:

Das absolute Ich kann man auch das Absolut synthetische Ich nennen. Es ist die Synthese des Ich, inwiefern es keine eigentliche Synthese ist — jedoch zum Behuf des Analytischen Ich so genannt werden muss, weil Analyse, indem es Analyse ist, sich nur Synthese entgegensetzen kann. Diese Synthese ist absolute Sfäre ohne Gränze — alle andre Synthesen sind relative Sphären i.e. Sfäre und Gränze zugleich. Sie enthält die Möglichkeit der Grenze überhaupt, im analytischen Ich. Das analytische Ich überhaupt erfüllt das Synthetische Ich. Das leztere ist die Sfäre des Analytischen — Sein Eins und Alles. Das synthetische Ich ist die nothwendige Substanz — das analytische die Mögliche und wirckliche — Ersteres in Beziehung auf jene, lezteres in Beziehung auf sich (139, 32-140, 12).

The dialectic pattern Novalis employs for his schema of interrelation is definitely Fichtean, and with respect to the "Fichte Studies", Theodor Haering's thesis that Novalis anticipates Hegel is true only insofar as Fichte himself anticipates Hegel. Novalis does not attempt to go beyond the basic structure of the Fichtean position, as has just been outlined. He seeks merely to interpret, not to outdistance, and his interpretative efforts stay well within Fichte's system. The undeniable difference which exists nonetheless between Novalis' speculations and the *Wissenschaftslehre* stems from a variation in emphasis. For Fichte, the decisive aspect is the ego's absolute autonomy and the object's corresponding lack of it which manifests itself empirically as moral freedom. Novalis, on the other hand, is primarily concerned with the ego's absolute unity in its empirical manifestation as that common point of balanced neutrality which alone guarantees the harmonious correspondence of subject and object. The harmonious correspondence of outer world and inner world is the ego's absolute heritage, and it constitutes the basis of all that we call experience; but only after the ego experiences those two worlds for what they are, namely one, has it really come into its heritage. That is the magic moment when subject and object are one, that is the homecoming promised in the famed answer to the question, "where are we going?" and that is the lifting of the veil at Sais which separated self from self. Fichte conceives of the relation between subject and object as a self-imposed limitation designed to be a constant challenge to the ego's autonomy, and to be challenged in its turn with equal constancy by that autonomy's empirical manifestation, by the freedom of moral action. Fichte views the empirical dichotomy of subject and object from the perspective of the ego's absolute autonomy which demands the ultimate elimination of the object. Since, however, the empirical state, as opposed to the Absolute, is characterized by the dualism of subject and object, the demand for the latter's subsumption under the former can be nothing but a directive which is never fulfilled. The 'Categorical Imperative' is that directive; it is the eternal 'ought to' according to which the subject acts in a determinative manner on its environment. Such action is called ethical action, and during its performance the subject functions as a free agent whereas the object assumes a state of complete dependency. An ethical act is, obviously, merely a transitory manifestation of the absolute law of unity according to which it takes place. The basic empirical dichotomy of subject and object persists, so that the empirical realm is ultimately characterized as the subject's ever unfulfilled striving to realize that unity which its absolute nature demands.

To Novalis unity means harmony rather than strife. The ego's absolute nature is not so much categorical demand, as it is source of the empirical state per se, and as such manifest in the very existence of that state. The empirical dichotomy of subject and object is possible only as the manifestation of absolute unity, and as this manifestation, subject and object are really one. Subject and object exist in a harmonious relationship so that one is the exact image of the other, or rather each is representative of the other.

With the mentioning of representative action, the next topic has already been stated. The third chapter deals with Novalis' concept of representation as the dynamic aspect of the schema of inter-relation which was outlined in the second chapter. The beginning of the second chapter already contains implicitly what the entire third chapter treats explicitly. The very concept of representation is basic to the notions of negative theology which, as we have stated, Novalis employs. If we say B is representative of A, then we mean that B circumscribes A negatively, *i.e.,* in terms other than A, and that it, therefore, can never BE A, or: the empirical is representative of the Absolute which means that the empirical circumscribes the Absolute negatively, *i.e.*, in terms other than the Absolute, and the empirical can, therefore, never BE the Absolute; one is the complete 'other' of the other. In terms of Novalis' schema, representation means the mutually representative reciprocity between the sub-jective and ojective realms which is representative of those realms' basic unity in the empirical ego, and the empirical ego's unity in its state of duplicity is representative of absolute unity. Fichte's abso-lute act of self-limitation is understood as self-representation by Novalis. The Ego leaves its identity in order to become represen-tative of its own self, and it does this by entering a state of non-identity, a state of duplicity which has previously been introduced as the dichotomy of subject and object. The state of duplicity must reenact the same process if it is to be representative of the Ego's action. This is accomplished insofar as each member of the dicho-tomy leaves its identity in order to become manifest in the other, and the mutually representative relation between subject and ob-ject returns the state of non-identity to its opposite, the state of

identity. Novalis' concept of representation can now be expressed
by this formula: the absolute ego and the empirical ego are in a
state of mutual representation insofar as subject and object stand
in an equally harmonious relation to one another.

Man's true home is the point of harmony between subject and
object. To reach it he has to travel both paths simultaneously, as
Novalis recommends. The agility necessary for this difficult under-
taking is to be earned through practice in the reenactment of the
very process on which the harmony between subject and object is
founded. In the act of artistic self-representation that harmony between subject and object is realized which ultimately underlies all
human existence, so that the terms man and artist become synonymous for Novalis.

Theodor Haering has already pointed out that the concept of
representative action is fulcral to Novalis' speculations. He, however, visualizes the representative interrelation between the Absolute and its manifestations along Hegelian lines, and as a result the
decisive factor of Novalis' Fichtean heritage, the central importance
of the ego in our interpretation of his schema of representative interrelation, is lost. The question whether Fichtean concepts dominate
Novalis' thoughts to a greater or lesser degree would in itself be
mere pedantry were it not that the accessibility of those very
thoughts depends largely on an accurate answer to it. The following
chapters constitute an attempt to pave the way in the direction of
finding that answer.

II

THE EGO: A SCHEMA OF INTERRELATION

Any attempt at systematizing Novalis' thought, especially that of the developmental stage from 1795 to 1796, is at best illusory, and the following pages did not spring from the desire to create such an illusion. Hans-Joachim Mähl's outstanding scholarship as editor of the "Fichte Studies" has enabled him to rearrange the entire body of early fragments in a manner most likely to reflect the original sequence in which they had been written.[1] It is undeniable that the individual blocks of fragmentary speculations seem to connect with a degree of coherence far superior to that of any previous edition; nonetheless, the "Fichte Studies" fail the reader who expects systematic clarity of expression. The power of these fragments lies not so much in their objective certainty, but rather, truly in accordance with the intellectual climate of that time, in their appeal to a subjective criterion. Fichte never tires to impress on his audience the necessity of reenacting those thought processes for which the words in his philosophical tracts are merely signposts; he rests the certainty of his philosophical arguments entirely with each individual's ability to do intellectually exactly as he does:

Die Wissenschaftslehre ist von der Art, dass sie durch den blossen Buchstaben gar nicht, sondern dass sie lediglich durch den Geist sich mittheilen lässt; weil ihre Grund-Ideen in jedem, der sie studirt, durch die schaffende Einbildungskraft selbst hervorgebracht werden müssen; wie es denn bei einer auf die letzten Gründe der menschlichen Erkenntniss zurückgehenden Wissenschaft nicht anders seyn konnte, indem das ganze Geschäft des menschlichen Geistes von der Einbildungskraft ausgeht, Einbildungskraft aber nicht anders, als durch Einbildungskraft aufgefasst werden kann (*SW*, I, 284).

[1] Kl², II.

It is reasonable to assume that Novalis' fragments constitute subjective exercises in accordance with this Fichtean exhortation which
would in part explain the strange ambivalence of his style.[2] The
variety of topics to be found in the "Fichte Studies" can be considered a repetition of the same thought process from numerous
points of perspective with the implied directive to any potential
reader that he is to re-perform that very process himself. The basic
appeal issued by the *Wissenschaftslehre* is: think a particular object, A, and observe your action in doing so. The same attitude of
self-examination also sets the tone throughout Novalis' fragments,
and it is the vantage point from which he reinvestigates the major
philosophic issues of his day.[3]

The only possible object of such scrutiny is the ego itself. The
form this scrutiny takes in the "Fichte Studies" has already been
described in the introductory chapter. There we had occasion to
observe that Novalis examines a number of basic dichotomies
which all stand ultimately for the ego in its state of constant self-
confrontation as subject and object. Fichte begins his investigation

[2] The best illustration of the effect this ambivalence can have would be
Carlyle's essay on Novalis. Despite his admitted inability to comprehend
much of what Novalis says, he cannot escape the attraction this author
nonetheless holds for him. Thomas Carlyle, "Novalis", *Critical and Miscellaneous Essays* (London, 1899).

[3] An explicit demonstration of this method can be found in these sentences
which lead into an examination concerning the nature of philosophy: "Welches ist aber ihr" (der Philosophie) "eigentlicher Wirkungskreis? Keine ge-
lehrte Kunst kann es nicht seyn. Sie muss nicht von Gegenständen und Kennt-
nissen abhängen, die erworben werden müssen — von einer Quantität der
Erfahrung — sonst wäre jede Wissenschaft Filosofie. Wenn also jene Wis-
senschaften sind, so ist sie keine. Was könnte es wohl seyn? Sie handelt von
einem Gegenstande, der nicht gelernt wird. Wir müssen aber alle Gegen-
stände lernen — Also von gar keinem Gegenstande. Was gelernt wird
muss doch verschieden seyn von dem Lernenden. Was gelernt wird ist
ein Gegenstand — also ist das Lernende kein Gegenstand. Könnte also die
Filosofie vielleicht vom Lernenden handeln, also von uns, wenn wir Gegen-
stände lernen? Die Filosofie ist aber selbst im Lernenden. Nun da wird sie
Selbstbetrachtung seyn. Ey! wie fängt es der Lernende an sich selbst in
dieser Operation zu belauschen. Er müsste sich also lernen — denn unter
lernen verstehn wir überhaupt nichts, als den Gegenstand anschauen und
ihn mit seinen Merckmale[n] uns einprägen. Es würde also wieder ein Gegenstand. Nein Selbstbetrachtung kann sie nicht seyn, denn sonst wäre sie nicht
das Verlangte. Es ist ein Selbstgefühl vielleicht. Was ist denn ein Gefühl . . ."
(113, 7-26).

of the ego with the sentence of identity, A = A, which is his way
of asking in the most abstract manner possible: what is the relationship between object and subject? Novalis asks the same question in
less abstract formulations when he juxtaposes form (*Form*) and
content (*Gehalt, Stoff*), inner (*innen*) and outer (*aussen*), time (*Zeit*)
and space (*Raum*), intellectual perception (*Vorstellung*) and sense
perception (*Anschauung*), analysis (*Analyse*) and synthesis (*Synthese*), and others. Fichte tracks down systematically the implications inherent in the sentence of identity, and the result is the
Wissenschaftslehre, a system subdivided into a theoretical and a
practical part. With Novalis neither method nor results are systematic. The "Fichte Studies" are not geared to furnish a system
which traces every aspect of the empirical manifold to its absolute
origin; they do, however, constitute their author's most strenuous
effort aimed at grasping the pure abstractions of Fichte's system
in terms more akin to immediate experience.

Fichte presents a system evolved from basic axioms; Novalis
traces the pattern of interrelation which underlies all apparent
dualism in the empirical realm by examining the prime dualism of
subject and object from a variety of perspectives. The present
chapter will reconstruct Novalis' concept of the basic schema of
interrelation between subject and object as it appears outlined
against the background of the diverse topics contained in the
"Fichte Studies". It must be remembered that Novalis writes his
fragments in an attempt to rethink the thoughts which gave birth
to the *Wissenschaftslehre.* He, therefore, accepts the basic framework of Fichte's philosophy. For Fichte anything empirical, in-
cluding the fundamental confrontation between ego and non-ego,
ultimately originates with the absolute ego, the realm of pure action
or self-enactment where there is no longer any foreign element to
create a difference between enactment and accomplishment. Novalis, too, cannot consider the prime empirical dichotomy of subject
and object without referring its apparent dualism to a ground of
absolute unity. Novalis' ideas on the relationship between subject
and object are thus dependent on his conceptualization of the Absolute. Therefore, this chapter's discussion of Novalis' schema of
the interrelation between subject and object will have to begin with
an outline of Novalis' concept of absolute values.

A. NOVALIS' NEGATIVE APPROACH TO ABSOLUTE VALUES

It is well known that the objective certainty of the laws of nature became untenable under the attacks of skeptics such as Hume. Thereupon, beginning with Kant's *Critiques,* the subject began to be explored as source of certainty which meant ascribing spontaneity to it. If this trend is followed through in its implications, the absolute spontaneity pre-Kantian metaphysics had ascribed to the Creator-God will accordingly be attributed to the ego. Thus the previous relation God-universe becomes that of absolute ego-empirical ego for Fichte. Novalis is fully aware of the religious implications of Fichtean philosophy when he says: "Die bisherigen Begriffe von Gott waren ziemlich richtige Ideen vom Menschen qua Intelligenz./" (290, 12-13). This awareness introduces a degree of caution toward the ego-concept which has often caused interpreters to conclude that Novalis was in basic disagreement with Fichte's philosophy. "Hat Fichte nicht zu willkührlich alles ins Ich hineingelegt? mit welchem Befugniss?" (107, 25-26). These are the words most frequently quoted in support of this view. Their meaning, however, is more that of a warning against oversimplification by a potentially misleading terminology rather than an outright questioning of the philosophical implications. If we consider the contextual environment from which this fragment is taken, then it immediately becomes apparent that Novalis is evaluating the amount of meaning the term 'ego' (*Ich*) can convey. Nothing is further from his mind than to do battle with the concept the Fichtean Ego stands for. The fifth fragment in its entirety reads:

Was verstehn wir unter Ich?
    Hat Fichte nicht zu willkührlich alles ins Ich hineingelegt? mit welchem Befugniss?
    Kann ein Ich sich als *Ich* setzen, ohne ein anderes Ich oder Nichtich - / Wie sind Ich und Nichtich gegensetzbar / (107, 24-28).

The opening line, which may be regarded as the heading for fragments five to eight, makes it quite clear that not the actual powers of the ego but rather the term 'ego' and the associations connected with it are to be discussed. Accordingly, Novalis goes on to question the sufficiency of Fichte's terminology, since he doubts that the term 'ego' can be expressive of 'everything' (*alles*), or, in other words, since he doubts that the term 'ego' can be expressive of an absolute value. The words which follow make it certain that Novalis is questioning the sufficiency of Fichte's terminology not in order to suggest the possibility of a better choice, but in order to state the insufficiency of any one term to convey absolute meaning. Novalis' rhetorical question, "Can an ego posit itself as an ego without positing another ego or non-ego?" ("Kann ein Ich sich als *Ich s*etzen, ohne ein anderes Ich oder Nichtich -"), means in language not forged by the *Wissenschaftslehre* that the entity which presents itself to our consciousness as ego never appears in a pure state, and any reference to it cannot constitute a reference to absolute values. The fragment ends with the question: "How can ego and non-ego be put in opposition to one another?" ("/Wie sind Ich und Nichtich gegensetzbar/"), which is a negative way of circumscribing the absolute function which Fichte refers to in positive terms as absolute ego or simply as Ego.

The next fragment ("Das Ich hat eine hieroglyphystische Kraft", 107, 29) continues to emphasize that Fichte's use of the term 'ego' is potentially misleading. Novalis' laconic statement loses some of its mystery if it is interpreted in connection with the following passage from Fichte's tract, *Von der Sprachfähigkeit und dem Ursprung der Sprache:*[4] "Die Natur offenbart sich uns besonders durch Gesicht und Gehör ... So wie die Natur den Menschen etwas durch Gehör und Gesicht bezeichnete, gerade so mussten sie es einander durch Freiheit bezeichnen. — Man könnte eine auf diese Grundregel aufgebaute Sprache die *Ur-* oder *Hieroglyphensprache* nennen."[5]

If Novalis' statement concerning the ego's hieroglyphic power ("Das Ich hat eine hieroglyphystische Kraft") is read with Fichte's definition of 'hieroglyphic language' (*Hieroglyphensprache*) in

---

[4]   The editors of Kl², II, point in their commentary (*Anmerkungen,* p. 724, No. 108, line 16 ff.) to this particular Fichtean tract in connection with Novalis' discussion of the concept 'sign' which follows almost directly upon the fragments just quoted.

[5]   *SW*, VIII, 309-310.

mind, then it may be reinterpreted to mean: Since all terms have binding significance only insofar as signs are a product born of freedom, the significant term 'ego', which may be called a hieroglyphic, must not be confused or equated with that which experience calls ego. In other words, Novalis warns against the confusion of experiential and significant values which can occur when the source of all communication is sought in experience rather than in the freely creative act mentioned by Fichte when he speaks of his language of hieroglyphics (*Hieroglyphensprache*).

The summary meaning to be derived from fragments five and six could now be expressed in the following paraphrase: What does the term 'ego' really mean? Did Fichte overload this term when he ascribed absolute spontaneity to it? The consciously experienced ego certainly has no such powers. In order to avoid being misled by Fichte's terminology, it must be remembered that for Fichte the significance of any term is based on a free act which takes primacy over any experiential data. Fichte is, therefore, justified in the use of his terminology, but it is nonetheless misleading and insufficient.

The alternative Novalis suggests can be found in the eighth fragment: "D[ie] Handlung, dass Ich sich als Ich sezt muss mit der Antithese eines unabhängigen Nichtich und der Beziehung auf eine sie umschliessende Säre verknüpft seyn — diese Säre kann man Gott und Ich nennen" (107, 32-108, 2). This fragment can best be interpreted if it is viewed in connection with the topic raised by fragment number six where the problematic relation between sign and object was broached. Within the Fichtean framework, which Novalis deals with in these fragments, sign and object correspond insofar as both are products of free action. Free action itself is absolute and is no product; it cannot, therefore, be an object, and no possible sign could ever correspond to it. Since free action manifests itself in two products, a summary term for either product could function as sign for the empirical manifestation of free action. The term for the determinative force of objectivity would be God, and the corresponding expression for subjective spontaneity Ego. The possibility of employing both terms with equal justification signifies that no term is fully expressive of the Absolute per se. For Novalis, the Absolute is thus a value which can be circumscribed only negatively; it is a negative principle in the same sense as the Divine is a negative principle for Dionysius Areopagitus.[6]

Throughout the "Fichte Studies" the reader finds a cautious hesitation whenever the author discovers that he is dealing with absolute values, and, in many instances, their negativity with respect to positive knowledge is directly stated. A very clear definition of what Novalis understands by the term 'ego' appears in these words which also most convincingly verify our interpretation of fragments five to eight:

Ich bedeutet jenes negativ zu erkennende Absolute - was nach aller Abstraction übrig bleibt - Was nur durch Handeln erkannt werden kann und was sich durch ewigen Mangel realisirt (270, 28-30).

Novalis speaks here of the absolute ego, of Fichte's Ego, in terms which leave no possibility of doubt that the Absolute is indeed a negative principle for him. The *via negativa,* which Haering believes to be of such minor significance for Novalis,[7] is marked

---

[6] The *theologia negativa* (negative theology) of Dionysius Areopagitus or Pseudo-Dionysius, may be found in four treatises still extant of which only *Concerning the Divine Names* and *Concerning Mystic Theology* (Parker ed.; London, 1897) are directly concerned with the present reference.

[7] Theodor Haering's discussion of A = A (and a = a) is based on the assumption that identity is used here in its absolute sense and therefore refers to the Absolute itself. He denies emphatically that the concepts of negative theology hold any definitive importance for Novalis: "In diesem Sinne ist wohl auch die sonst sehr dunkle Stelle II, 161 zu erklären, wo Novalis, (im Zusammenhang jener Diskussion des A = A in II, 159 ff.), von einem 'zweiten Weg' zur Bestimmung des Absoluten spricht, von dem aber zunächst namentlich nicht recht deutlich ist, ob derselbe für ihn nur etwas Ähnliches wie etwa Platons 'zweite Fahrt' bedeutet, von der dieser in seinen Nomoi im Gegensatz zu seiner Politeia als von einem vorläufigen Notbehelf redet, wenn der eigentliche erste und idealste Weg und das eigentliche letzte Ideal sich nicht realisieren lässt, oder ob er für ihn wirklich einen gleichberechtigten, zweiten Weg darstellt. Nach meiner Meinung ist das erstere der Fall. Novalis sagt hier: 'Oder wir stellen es (das Identische) durch ein Nichtsein (dar).' Während dies zunächst im Sinne der alten 'via negationis' in der Bestimmung des Absoluten aufgefasst werden könnte, also in dem Sinne, dass man von ihm — wie oben schon in Begriffen wie Un-endlichkeit, Un-bestimmtheit, usw. — nur alle Eigenschaften des bloss Gegenständlichen negiert, gibt die Fortsetzung ein Rätsel auf, indem Novalis hinzufügt: 'durch ein nichtidentisches Vorzeichen'. Am plausibelsten scheint mir die Deutung, dass damit auch nur jene Vorsilbe 'Un' gemeint ist, welche eben diesen Begriff als bloss gegenständlich und die wahre Identität nicht erfassend bezeichnet. Wie dem aber auch sein mag: falls die via negationis als solcher

precisely as the path along which the Absolute is to be approached. Again, contrary to Haering's overall interpretation, that Absolute is defined by Novalis, very much in accordance with Fichte's position, as 'ego'.

The Absolute has been defined as a negative principle, as a value which no positive term or concept can grasp, so that it can be approached on a negative path only. A brief outline of the characteristics which mark this path for Novalis must therefore complement the present definition of the Absolute as a negative principle. The most striking general example of the Absolute's manifestation as a negative principle would be the unity which, paradoxically enough, inheres within the infinite multiplicity of empirical phenomena. Each individual thing claims to be absolute merely by being that ONE thing. That claim is, however, constantly overruled by the fact that each thing is also related to all other things. The isolationist shell of singularity is broken each time a transition from one thing to another is made, and this can be done only by that which really is One and thus Absolute. No thing is the Thing, the final all inclusive unity, and this eternal 'no' is the only trace the Absolute leaves for us. The 'no's' are the negative markers which map out the path to the Absolute. In reflecting on the dynamics of philosophy, Novalis gives a clear view of this *via negativa:*

Filosofiren muss eine eigne Art von Denken seyn. Was thu ich, indem ich filosofire? ich denke über einen Grund nach. Dem Filosofiren liegt also ein Streben nach dem Denken eines Grundes zum Grunde. Grund ist aber nicht Ursache im eigentlichen Sinne - sondern innre Beschaffenheit - Zusammenhang mit dem Ganzen. Alles Filosofiren muss also bey einem absoluten Grunde endigen. Wenn dieser nun nicht gegeben wäre, wenn dieser Begriff eine Unmöglichkeit enthielte - so wäre der Trieb zu Filosophiren eine unendliche Thätigkeit - und darum ohne Ende, weil ein ewiges Bedürfniss nach einem absoluten Grunde vorhanden wäre, das doch nur relativ gestillt werden könnte - und darum

---

zweiter Weg gemeint ist, so ist er für Novalis eben doch wirklich nur ein Notbehelf, der das wahre Wesen der Identität nur ganz vage bezeichnet, während in dem A = A die Struktur desselben, wenn auch freilich nur eben indirekt, d.h. nur stellvertretend, aber eben doch positiv zum Ausdruck kommt" (p. 158). This interpretation is further invalidated by the improved rendering of this particular quotation in Kl², II, where it reads: "— Oder wir stellen es durch sein Nichtseyn, durch ein Nichtidentisches vor — Zeichen . . ." (104, 10-11).

nie aufhören würde. Durch das freywillige Entsagen des Absoluten entsteht die unendliche freye Thätigkeit in uns - das Einzig mögliche Absolute, was uns gegeben werden kann und was wir nur durch unsre Unvermögenheit ein Absolutes zu erreichen und zu erkennen, finden. Dies uns gegebne Absolute lässt sich nur negativ erkennen, indem wir handeln und finden, dass durch kein Handeln das erreicht wird, was wir suchen (269, 23-270, 6).

Even though Novalis' formulations definitely express a trend found in the tradition of Christian mysticism, none of the writings from Denis the Areopagite to Jakob Böhme need be the primary source for his 'negative theology'. Both Kant and Fichte make full use of negative principles which fulfill a regulative function. The Kantian term 'idea' (*Idee*) signifies a unity transcending that of the categories; it is as such inconceivable except as guideline for coherence within the conceivable realm.[8] The Categorical Imperative, for instance, is the purely regulatory manifestation of the absolute ego as the principle of duty common to all men yet never fully demonstrable in any one or any number of actions.

Fichte comments in these words on the Categorical Imperative:

So wie das Ich gesetzt ist, ist alle Realität gesetzt; im Ich soll alles gesetzt seyn; das Ich soll schlechthin unabhängig, Alles aber soll von ihm abhängig seyn. Also, es wird die Übereinstimmung des Objects mit dem Ich gefordert; und das absolute Ich, gerade um seines absoluten Seyns willen, ist es, welches sie fordert.*
*Kants kategorischer Imperativ. Wird es irgendwo klar, dass Kant seinem kritischen Verfahren, nur stillschweigend, gerade die Prämissen zu Grunde legt, welche die Wissenschaftslehre aufstellt, so ist es hier. Wie hätte er jemals auf einen kategorischen Imperativ, als absolutes Postulat der Übereinstimmung mit dem reinen Ich, kommen können, ohne aus der Voraussetzung eines absoluten Seyns des Ich, durch welches alles gesetzt wäre, und, inwiefern es nicht *ist*, wenigstens seyn *solle*. - Kants mehrste Nachfolger scheinen das, was sie über den kategorischen Imperativ sagen, diesem grossen Manne bloss nachzusagen, und über den Grund der Befugniss, eines absoluten Postulats noch nicht aufs reine gekommen zu seyn. - Nur *weil*, und *inwiefern* das Ich

---

[8] C.f., Kant, *Kritik der reiner Vernunft* (p. 244) or Eisler's *Kant Lexikon* (pp. 257-264). Karl Jaspers furnishes a most precise summary on the Kantian doctrine of ideas in the final chapter of his *Psychologie der Weltanschauungen* (3rd ed.; Berlin, 1925). Under the heading "Kants Ideenlehre" he clarifies the purely regulative nature which Kant attributes to his concept of the idea (*Idee*).

selbst absolut ist, hat es das Recht, absolut zu postuliren; und dieses Recht erstreckt sich denn auch nicht weiter, als auf ein Postulat dieses seines absoluten Seyns, aus welchem denn freilich noch manches andere sich dürfte *deduciren* lassen (*SW*, I, 260).

Furthermore, for Fichte both theoretical and practical action of the empirical ego is regulated by the 'idea' of the absolute ego which is as such neither object of consciousness nor ever the realizable goal of practical endeavors:

Dadurch haben wir endlich auch den gesuchten Vereinigungspunct zwischen dem absoluten, praktischen und intelligenten Wesen des Ich gefunden. - Das Ich fordert, dass es alle Realität in sich fasse, und die Unendlichkeit erfülle. Dieser Forderung liegt nothwendig zum Grunde die Idee des schlechthin gesetzten, unendlichen Ich; und dieses ist das *absolute* Ich, von welchem wir geredet haben. (Hier erst wird der Sinn des Satzes: *das Ich setzt sich selbst schlechthin,* völlig klar. Es ist in demselben gar nicht die Rede von dem in wirklichen Bewusstseyn gegebenen Ich; denn dieses ist nie schlechthin, sondern sein Zustand ist immer, entweder unmittelbar, oder mittelbar durch etwas ausser dem Ich begründet; sondern von einer Idee des Ich, die seiner praktischen unendlichen Forderung nothwendig zu Grunde gelegt werden muss, die aber für unser Bewusstseyn unerreichbar ist, und daher in demselben nie unmittelbar [wohl aber mittelbar in der philosophischen Reflexion] vorkommen kann) (*SW*, I, 277).

Novalis certainly gives evidence of being especially attracted by the concept 'regulative' as it appears with Kant in this connection;[9] also, in his attempt to come to terms with the concept 'ego' we find it employed:

Ich - ist vielleicht, wie alle Vernunftideen blos regulativen, classificiren-den Gebrauchs - Gar nicht in Beziehung zur Realität (258, 18-19).

---

[9] There are numerous references in which the term 'regulative' appears; just to name a few within this context: "Wir müssen die Idee nicht verfolgen, denn sonst kommen wir in die Räume des Unsinns — Jede regulative Idee ist von unendlichen Gebrauch" (252, 5-7); "Alles Suchen nach der Ersten" (Gattung) "ist Unsinn — es ist *regulative Idee*" (254, 11-12); "Die ganze Filo-sofie ist nur Wissenschaft der Vernunft — blos zu regulativen Gebrauch — lediglich ideal — ohne die mindeste Realität im eigentlichen Sinne" (256, 19-21); "Was verstehn wir unter dem Vorstellenden? Die Szene der Vor-stellung, oder ihre Ursache — Ursache aber ist nur ein regulativer Begriff, eine Vernunftidee — es wäre also thöricht ihr reale Wircksamkeit beyzu-legen. Wir suchen also ein Unding" (255, 11-14).

Not only do these words emphasize once more that Novalis thinks of the Ego as a negative principle, but they also express quite clearly the positive manner in which such a principle may make itself manifest. The Absolute manifests itself as *regula,* as a rule or law. The full implications of Novalis' point of view become more apparent if the concept of law is briefly explained in general terms. By the force of a law, otherwise unrelated multiples become interdependent and thus one; yet no single demonstration of that law nor any sum of demonstrations will ever be the final and exhaustive demonstration of that law itself. The concept law actually stands for a paradox: it stands for unity within multiplicity. It will become apparent that Novalis thinks of the absolute ego as manifest in the law which binds subject and object together. The law in question is the law of identity which is founded on the ego's simultaneous inherence in subject and object.

Let us now summarize Novalis' views on the Absolute and its relation to the empirical realm as they were presented in this chapter. It will then become clear that the Absolute, be its name God or Ego, makes itself manifest as the relationship between subject and object, and it is this relationship rather than any finite entity which constitutes the empirical ego.

The Absolute is never identifiable with any one of the parts related by virtue of it; related multiplicity is as such different from absolute unity. Just as God cannot be identified with His creation and much less with any particular creature, the absolute ego is not identifiable with the subject, and much less with any of the subject's particular states of being affected by objects. Both God and Ego are concepts which signify empirically the interrelation between 'same' and 'other' or self and world, subject and object. If in the empirical interrelation between subject and object external objectivity is felt to be causal, absolute unity will be conceived of as a deity whose law inheres in the physical universe of which the self is a part. If, on the other hand, causality is found to be in the subject, the reverse is true. The self or subject is then experienced as the identity which unites objectivity by the laws of knowledge. If the point of departure for deriving the absolute unity implied in the interrelation between subject and object is objectivity, the resultant Absolute will bear the mark which characterizes objectivity for the subject, the mark of otherness. The Absolute under the aspect of complete otherness would be that which Novalis called God ("diese Sfäre kann man Gott und Ich nennen", 108, 2), and it will be the UNIFORM source of MULTIPLICITY. But objectivity under the aspect of its relatedness to the subject is not at all the complete 'other'; rather, it is both other and self, thing and thing experienced, so that the characteristic of otherness is actually accompanied by the characteristic of sameness. If, on the other hand, the subject is the point of departure, the Absolute will bear the mark which characterizes subjectivity for the subject, the mark of identity. The Absolute under the aspect of identity would be that which Novalis called Ego ("Diese Sfäre kann man Gott und Ich nennen"). The subject, however, proves not to be identical with itself insofar as it is related to the object, so that the characteristic of sameness is actually accompanied by the characteristic of otherness. In both cases the seemingly solid lines of demarcation which define the subject and the object fade away, a fact which Novalis expresses as "Der *Mensch* ist so gut Nichtich, als Ich" (268, 24).

The paradox that man leads a dual existence as subject and object may become clearer if we also consider the following pronouncement made by Novalis: "Das Subject ist *zugleich* Ganzes und Theil. - Daher seine Abstammung vom Absoluten Ich, oder von sich selbst" (134, 24-25). Here Novalis views the paradoxical interrelation betweeen subject and object under the category of unity. The underlined term 'simultaneously' (*zugleich*) signifies the binding force, the law, which unites the empirical ego's subjective and objective moments, its aspects of wholeness and partiality. Novalis states in effect that absolute unity manifests itself empirically as the relative unity between subject and object. Empirically the concept of unity is dualistic: it can be either part or whole and the empirical perspective of the Absolute will be determined by that very dualism so that the Absolute will also appear under the same twofold aspect. We had come to know it as 'God' and 'Ego'; both terms stand for absolute unity of which, per definition, there can only be one. The prime empirical reality is the self, the individual 'I', that which Novalis called 'man' (*Mensch*), and it constitutes in its simultaneous function as physical part and spiritual whole of the universe ('Das Subject ist *zugleich* Ganzes und Theil", 134, 24) the empirical point of perspective from which the Absolute appears as God and as absolute ego, respectively.

If man envisions himself as part of an infinite multiplicity external to himself, then the concept of God designates the absolute unity which manifests itself as the regulative principle by means of which thing relates to thing in that infinite multiplicity. If, on the other hand, man envisions himself as knower of a potentially infinite multiplicity of objects, then the concept of the absolute ego stands for that very same absolute unity; in this case, however, absolute unity manifests itself as the regulative principle which unites in the ego's experience of self-identity the ego's unlimited states of being affected by the knowledge of objects. Since two points of perspective, one directed at infinity external and the other directed at infinity internal, are both possible to man, and, more than that, must even be held simultaneously by him, Novalis is quite justified in regarding the concepts God and Ego[10] as equivalents. God and Ego are different terms for absolute unity pure and simple. The difference in terminology arises with the twofold perspective from which the Absolute is perceived empirically. Absolute unity, the Absolute itself, is for Novalis a purely negative value, never to be perceived directly as One and, therefore, manifest only as the relative unity between the empirical ego's subjective and objective aspects; never to be expressed by any one name, and, therefore, entitled either 'God' or 'Ego' according to the perspective from which it is viewed.

B.   NOVALIS' CONCEPT OF UNITY

1. *Unity in General*

The foundation for the outline of Novalis' basic schema of interrelation has now been established. We were able to define the point of unity between subject and object as the empirical ego in its binary relation to the Absolute on a subjective and an objective basis. We

---

[10]   "D[ie] Handlung, dass Ich sich als Ich sezt muss mit der Antithese eines unabhängigen Nichtich und der Beziehung auf eine sie umschliessende Sfäre verknüpft seyn — diese Sfäre kann man Gott und Ich nennen" (107, 32-108, 2).

have found, furthermore, that the concepts 'subject' and 'object' are only possible if we abstract from one or the other of the directions of perspective; in reality there is perfect simultaneity which results in the loss of the accustomed division of reality into the equations I = subject, world = object.

In the course of our investigation, it became evident that we had to rely increasingly on the concept of unity in order to interpret Novalis' ideas concerning the Absolute and its relation to the empirical realm. It has, therefore, become necessary to examine Novalis' concept of unity in more detail. The nature of this topic will require references to mathematics which, however, merely constitute analogical illustrations of the philosophical concepts under discussion. They are in no way concerned with Novalis' view of mathematics per se, especially since the "Fichte Studies" contain only very few entries directly related to that subject. Käte Hamburger has already emphasized in her outstanding essay, "Novalis und die Mathematik", that Novalis relies in his philosophical notions very heavily on ideas derived from higher mathematics. How close the concepts of calculus can be to what we have found to be the ego's binary relation to the Absolute becomes obvious in statements like these:

Dass Novalis, indem er den Menschen mit dem Punkt vergleicht und den Ursprung oder Keim einer unermesslichen Welt in ihm findet, indem er also die infinitesimale Erzeugungseinheit irgendwie im Menschen begründet sieht, wie bereits das Fragment III, 103 deutlich erkennen liess, tatsächlich an die Differential- und Integralrechnung denkt, erweist ein anderes Fragment, in dem er nun den Menschen selbst als Differential und Integral bezeichnet: "Sollte der Mensch die Einheit für die Natur, das Weltall sein i.e. das Differential der unendlich grossen und das Integral der unendlich kleinen Natur, das allgemein homogeneisierende Prinzip, das Mass aller Dinge, ihr Realisierungsprinzip, das Organ ihres Kontakts"? * Die Einheit, die das Bewusstsein für die gesamte gegenständliche Welt gewährleistet, vom Unendlichgrossen bis zum Unendlichkleinen in kontinuierlichem Zusammenhang, wird hier auf den Menschen, dessen Wesen sie prägt, übertragen, der als eine endliche Gesamtheit (Integral) und als eine unendlichkleine Grösse (Differential) je nach dem Standpunkt in einem tieferen Sinne als dem des blossen Gleichnisses gesehen wird.

* III, 102. Auch die Relativität der unendlichen Grösse wird hier ausgesprochen. Der Punkt (vergleichsweise der Mensch) wird hier nicht

als absoluter Ursprung bezeichnet, sondern kann in Bezug auf eine andere Ordnung als Integral gelten (pp. 152-153).

Since the bulk of Käte Hamburger's material is taken from fragments which were written after 1796, it seems particularly noteworthy, and indicative of the decisive position the "Fichte Studies" hold for Novalis' intellectual development, that central concepts formulated in these early speculations obviously maintained their validity for the author in his later philosophical endeavors.

The concept of unity, for instance, definitely appears already in the early fragments as a functional relationship of the kind Käte Hamburger describes. The sophisticated mathematical terminology is still lacking, yet the need to use mathematical imagery in order to come to grips with philosophical complexities makes itself felt decisively throughout the "Fichte Studies". Prominent amongst the imagery used is the concept of the circle. Novalis employs it when he is confronted with the task of illustrating that the particular dichotomy he happens to be discussing is ultimately dependent on the prerequisite of unity. As important as the concept of unity and the concept of its geometrical representative are to the "Fichte Studies" in general, no clear definition of either is ever given on its own terms. We have, for example, already encountered the concept of the absolute sphere which links ego and non-ego ("D[ie] Handlung, dass Ich sich als Ich sezt muss mit der Antithese eines unabhängigen Nichtich und der Beziehung auf eine sie umschliessende Sfäre verknüpft seyn — ", 107, 32-108, 1). Pronouncements like these, which actually deal with problems of a more specific nature, furnish the only information on Novalis' ideas concerning unity and circularity. In the statement above Novalis discusses the ego, and unity happens to be an essential aspect of the discussion. In a like manner, we shall encounter the concepts of unity and circularity as an integral part of the topics still to be discussed.

Since Novalis does not explain the concept of unity on its own terms, any attempt at furnishing the definition of unity for the "Fichte Studies" would necessarily have to be an interpretation derived from the entire body of fragments. If, as in the fragment just cited, references to the all-inclusive sphere on which the interrelation between ego and non-ego depends are to be understood, a general interpretation of Novalis' concept of unity must be offered at this point.[11]

The concept 'one' as a unit signifies nothing else but the common point of origin for two progressions toward infinity in opposite directions. Any one object can expand into infinity as the beginning part of an infinite progression into the objective realm; it can also furnish the starting point of a progression toward infinity in reverse which is also known as infinite regression; or, "Jedes Ding ist einer allgemeinen und einer besondern Entgegensetzung fähig" (234, 16-17), which is equivalent to: "Jede Sache kann im Verhältniss zu sich selbst, und zu sich nicht selbst betrachtet werden" (111, 24-25). Novalis uses the terms 'synthesis' (*Synthese*) and 'analysis' (*Analyse*) when he refers to the ego's binary extension. Since those concepts are not easily explained in a few words and constitute, moreover, the topic of an entire section later on in this chapter, we shall employ the terms 'progression' and 'regression' as auxiliary expressions for the time being.

The concept 'infinity' in its negative circumscription signifies 'no limit' which excludes all aspects of 'otherness'; positively speaking, 'infinity' signifies self-identity in its only possible form, and unity in its absolute form. Self-identity, One, Absolute and 'infinity' are, therefore, different aspects of one and the same concept.

Opposites are one in two respects: (1) on their mutual limiting ground, and there, the emphasis of their relationship is on their otherness; (2) with respect to their common circumference, and there, the emphasis of their relationship is on their identity and oneness. Novalis defines the relationship between opposites in these words: "Zwey Entgegengesezte haben ein gleiches und ein Entgegengeseztes Merckmal — und beide in Konnexion" (227, 20-21).

Any one object in its capacity as mutual starting point for an

---

[11]   Dietrich Mahnke states at the beginning of his excellent study, *Unendliche Sphäre und Allmittelpunkt* (Halle, 1937), that Novalis employs the concepts of 'infinite sphere' (*unendliche Sphäre*) and 'productive center' (*unerschöpflicher Mittelpunkt*), but he fails to explain those concepts in Novalis' terms. He offers instead a summary of the employment those symbols experienced, from the age of Romanticism to the time of ancient Greece. Nonetheless, his work proved to be a helpful guide to Novalis' theory of unity.

extension into external and internal infinity constitutes also a mutual limiting ground within an infinite continuum. The common circumference necessarily prerequisite to the establishment of such a ground would have to be the absolute unity of infinity. According to Novalis this unity is furnished by the consciousness within which the object is found: "Entgegensetzen ist stricte — vereinigen — indem beydes durch ein Drittes sich entgegen gesezt — aber dadurch in Einem Bewusstseyn vereinigt wird — " (240, 5-7).

To determine the center of the enclosing unity, the prime limiting ground has to be found, the ground which also functions as the mutual starting point for the dual progressions into infinity. For the Absolute only one such ground can exist: it would be the starting point for both progressions towards infinity, a reference point for their respective rates of progress, and a reference point for their difference in direction.

Let us now illustrate geometrically what we have said of the all-enclosing unity and its center. We select a given point and establish it as the center of a circle from which two radii run into infinity along an angle of 180°. At any point along those radii, the circumference can be drawn and redrawn *ad infinitum*. The circumference can be drawn at any given point, because the initial point was designated 'center' which in turn was possible only by referring negatively to a circumference. The absolute circumference need not be stated in negative terms only. If the two radii are envisioned as emanating at an equal rate from a common center in opposite directions, then they would constitute an ever present yet ever expanding circumference, a circumference infinite and absolute. All stations along a line of progress are fixed with respect to its beginning and end. If the beginning is the only defined point, then all further points derive their definedness from this initial point, whereas undefined infinity furnishes the aspect of direction.

Since consciousness is the enclosing unity of all things, its only unvarying object would also be the fixed point of origin which serves as the mutual limiting ground as well as the starting point for the two progressions toward the infinite. The only unvarying object of consciousness is the self, or the ego, and it is, therefore, the center of the sphere of consciousness. The ego in its objective existence as "I the individual" constitutes the initial moment for

the dual progression into infinity, whereas the ego in its absolute
existence as "I, consciousness which never becomes object" constitutes the infinity which is both prerequisite and goal of those
progressions. Novalis envisions the very same relationship between
the absolute and the empirical ego when he says:

Das absolute Ich geht vom Unendlichen zum Endlichen, das mittelbare
Ich vom Endlichen zum Unendlichen. Wie kommt aber das absolute
Ich ins Endliche, wo es sodann nach seinem eignen Gesetze mittelbares
Ich wird? Das absolute Ich ist Eins und getheilt zugleich. Insofern es
getheilt ist muss es ein empirisches Bewusstseyn haben - kurz mittelbares Ich seyn. Das getheilte Ich muss doch verbunden seyn - und zwar
durch den Trieb Ich zu seyn. Das Ich muss getheilt seyn, um Ich zu
seyn - nur der Trieb Ich zu seyn vereinigt es - das unbedingte Ideal des
reinen Ich ist also das Characteristische des Ich überhaupt - (126, 28-
127, 3).

and more specifically, pointing to the circular image employed in
our explanation:

Ansch[auung] und Vorstellung scheinen mir zwar aufs strengste getrennt, aber in sofern Eins zu seyn - dass beyde dieselbe Linie, nur in
entgegengesezter Richtung sind. Diese Zirkellinie ist so gross und so
klein, als man will, es kommt ja nur auf die unendliche Theilbarkeit
und Theilung derselben an (190, 1-5).

It has become evident that the general discussion of the concept of
unity has inadvertently reverted to the more specific topic of the
ego. We have found that there is no unity but that of the absolute
ego: It is the beginning, because only through the absolute ego's
unity does the empirical ego derive the unity which enables it to
function as the center that leads into the dual expanse of the objective and the subjective realms or of the outer and the inner
worlds. It is also the end, because the absolute ego is the infinite
sphere whose circumference is the ever-beckoning goal of the subjective and the objective progressions into infinity. Unity and ego
are concepts which are identical for Novalis, and the present discussion on Novalis' concept of unity is best continued in terms
relative to the ego.

2. Unity in Terms of the Ego

The terms 'inner world' and 'outer world' are sufficiently familiar through common usage. They stand for the paradoxical dualism which is man, for his subjective and his objective states. Novalis describes the relationship between 'inner world' (*innre Welt*) and 'outer world' (*äussere Welt*) as one of perfect correspondence in a state of opposition, which is merely another way of saying dual progressions in opposite directions travelling at the same rate into infinity:

Unsre innre Welt muss der äussern durchaus, bis in die kleinsten Theile correspondiren - denn sie sind sich im Gantzen Entgegengesezt. Was sich dort so entgegengesetzt ist - ist sich hier umgekehrt entgegengesezt, oder durcheinander bestimmt - lauter antithetische Bestimmungen (293, 29-33).

If we analyze Novalis' words in detail and connect them with his concepts on unity which were outlined previously, we arrive at the following interpretation: The individual experiences itself as an 'inner' and as an 'outer' entity. Its outer self is the physical unit which extends into infinity as the determinant part of an unlimited objective realm. The seeming 'receptivity of the senses' is the extent of the ego's determinating function and establishes the standard rate of the assymptodic approach towards infinity. The movement towards infinity itself, however, accounts for the 'otherness' of each particular object and designates the supply of such objects as un-limited. The ego as 'start' of the progression functions as point of reference for any other point, and in this capacity establishes each point not only as different from itself but also as different from any other point. Each object is but a point of simultaneous reference to the ego and to the infinite. But the physical unit of the self is not only a determinant; it is also the basic objective entity in which capacity it functions as the prime part of the infinite totality. For this reason that aspect of the self experiences itself as governed by the empirical realm. Novalis calls the continuum, along which the progression from object to object extends into infinity, space: "Ge-trenntseyn d[urch] ein Verbundenseyn - Raum./" (137, 5)

The progression in the opposite direction has already been circumscribed by the term 'inner world'. Here the unit of the self stands for 'totality' rather than 'prime unit part', and the path towards infinity is one of infinite regression. The self functions in this respect as the vessel of an unlimited conceptualized universe regressing along a continuum which Novalis calls time: "/Verbundenseyn durch ein Getrenntseyn - Zeit" (137, 4). The categories of thought are the inner equivalent of the senses insofar as they determine the standard rate of regression, or in Novalis' words: "Die Kategorieen enthalten die ursprünglichen Eigenschaften der Gattung überhaupt und sind immer vorhanden — nur nicht als Object — sondern als Subject — Form und Materie des Objects und Zusammenhang zwischen allen" (252, 28-31). Since the initial point is 'totality', and since the ever increasing multiplicity within it derives its order and coherence from that very totality, the inner self is experienced in this respect as autonomous. The direction towards infinite multiplicity, however, is contrary to the simple unity of totality, and an element of 'otherness' is thus also present within the inner self. Each conceptualized object is, therefore, experienced as part of the self, yet as an 'other' than the experiencing self, nonetheless. Here again each conceptualized object constitutes a reference point simultaneously referring to the ego and the infinite. The difference is merely that the ego is considered under the aspect of totality rather than under the aspect of unit part.

In summary, then, Novalis views the interrelation between the inner and the outer worlds as a perfect correspondence with inverted values, that is to say, as a perfect mirror-effect. The inversion accounts for the element of difference or division so that the 'part' of one world becomes the 'whole' of the other ("Das Subject ist *zugleich* Ganzes und Teil -" 134, 24). The correspondence accounts for the element of sameness or unity so that the term 'empirical ego' signifies nothing else but the corresponding relation between the inner and the outer worlds ("Das Ich muss getheilt seyn, um Ich zu seyn — nur der Trieb Ich zu seyn vereinigt es — das unbedingte Ideal des reinen Ich ist also das Characteristische des Ich überhaupt —" 127, 1-3).

The interrelation between the various aspects of the ego has now been outlined. The function and place of the object, however, must still be filled in to complete the picture. No additional source material will be required for this purpose, since all the necessary information is already contained within our present findings. The task now is to reformulate our findings in a manner which will make apparent the object's function in the interplay between absolute ego and empirical ego.

The object constitutes a twofold relationship to unity which is effected in each of two instances in a direct and an indirect manner. The direct relationship is called 'empirical ego', and the indirect one infinity. 'Externally' the term object designates a direct relation to the unity as manifest in the unity of the part, which is the unity of the ego in its physical existence, and an indirect relation to the infinity of absolute totality. 'Internally' the term object designates a direct relation to unity as it is manifest in the unity of totality, which is the unity of the ego as perceptive agent, and an indirect relation to the infinity of absolute partiality. The ego constitutes the same dual relation to unity in a direct and an indirect manner of which there is only one instance, however, in contrast to the previous two. The indirect relation is called infinity, and it constitutes the positive manifestation of absolute unity in the relative fusion of its dual aspects of whole and part.

The ego stands in constant relation with its own self. It does so on a direct basis as empirical ego which signifies the union of the unitary aspects whole and part into one being. It also employs an objective medium for an indirect relation to itself. For the ego as unit part, the aspect of the ego's physical existence, the object is the medium by means of which the ego is related to the infinitely expandable totality of the universe. This is an indirect relationship insofar as this totality is never reached at any one point and, therefore, constitutes a negative value. The ego's spiritual nature is able to contain all that which it encounters physically, and thus the ego constitutes wholeness or totality which is able to contain an ever increasing content. Here, again, the object serves to relate in an indirect manner the ego's aspect of totality with its aspect of partiality, since the ego as part, that is, the conceptualized physical ego, will have to constitute the standard according to which the entire spiritual content will be measured; it is the basic divisor, so to speak, for the otherwise undifferentiated whole of consciousness. Here, too, we deal with a negative value, insofar as the ego as part never stays the same, but appears within consciousness as a continuous state of being affected. The unity which is, nonetheless, inherent in this infinite multiplicity is a manifestation of absolute unity which, in this function, can be equated to self-identity. Self-identity, per definition, is the Absolute, since it implies 'no other'.

The ego is unity, and it stands in a direct and indirect relation with itself. Its direct relation is called empirical ego, its indirect one is a two-directional extension along objectivity into infinity. The former constitutes, as the manifest unity between part and whole, the direct relation of the Absolute to the empirical and the latter, the indirect relation of the empirical to the Absolute.

The ego's basic characteristic is unity, despite its dualistic role as starting point for two infinite progressions in opposite directions. It is the MUTUAL starting point for the two progressions towards infinity, and it is that with respect to the absolute unity of the infinite towards which the progressions extend. If there were two infinites, they would constitute two Absolutes, *i.e.*: two 'unlimitables', and between them no relation at all would be possible so that no common aspect between the two starting points could possibly exist. In that case, the ego could never be conscious of its own self, since consciousness relates under its unity all it contains. All these possibilities are uniformly denied insofar as self-consciousness is inseparable from the ego. In its self-consciousness, the ego experiences itself as 'one'.

Except for the task of summarizing the results into a compact image of the newly evolved ego concept, our discussion of the rather complex thoughts which comprise Novalis' idea of unity has come to an end. Unity in the accustomed sense, as it is seemingly possessed by each and every object in its state of being a separate entity, does not exist. The unity of any particular object exists only insofar as that object relates to a subject, and the unity of the subject exists only insofar as the subject relates to a potential infinity of objects. The law of this reciprocity between subject and object is the actual unity from which the subject's and the object's relative unity is derived. This law is, in turn, derived from absolute unity per se. The ego exists empirically as both subject and object and it is the empirical ego which is the law of the exact correspondence between the 'inner' and the 'outer' worlds. The empirical ego is unity, not in the sense of an isolated unit but rather in the sense of a relation between opposites, and it is as this unifying function the only manifestation of the absolute unity which is the absolute ego.

If the reader is to visualize the ego's functions under the aspect of unity as clearly as possible, he will find it useful to employ a geometrical analogy and imagine the following: at first a circular circumference, then the center to his circumference, and finally, two radii directly opposed to one another extending at the same rate towards the circumference which they ultimately and simultaneously meet. All that need be done now is to eliminate the circumference, and the image will emerge of two separate radii extending into infinity, always in direct opposition, yet, at the same time, always one with respect to the all-encompassing circumference which is potentially present at any and all given points along their progression. Novalis has the image of these two radii in mind when he refers, in the words previously cited,[12] to the relation between the realm of thought (*i.e.*, thought perception, *Vorstellung*) and the realm of the senses (*i.e.*, sense perception, *Anschauung*), and it is the image which best illustrates the ever-present yet never realized absolute unity of the Ego as manifest relative unity.

The ego's direct relation to absolute unity, or rather to its own absolute self, the Ego, consists of its being the common ground for two progressions towards infinity in opposite directions, and these progressions constitute the ego's indirect relation to absolute unity. This, the ego's unity derived from the absolute unity insofar as it is by its mere existence designated 'starting point for the infinite progressions', is reflected in the unity of self-consciousness. Without self-consciousness the ego remains a mere dualism and would as such be neither starting point nor related to Unity in any way; it would be nothing, or rather it would not be.

---

[12]   "Ansch[auung] und Vorstellung scheinen mir zwar aufs strengste getrennt, aber in sofern Eins zu seyn — dass beyde dieselbe Linie, nur in entgegengesezter Richtung sind. Diese Zirkelline ist so gross und so klein, als man will, es kommt ja nur auf die unendliche Theilbarkeit und Theilung derselben an" (190, 1-5).

C. SYNTHESIS AND ANALYSIS

When Novalis refers to the ego's binary extensions, he frequently uses the terms 'synthesis' and 'analysis' rather than 'progression' and 'regression' which we have employed hitherto for the sake of simplicity. Now, however, it is necessary to return to Novalis' terminology in order to expose the conceptualization underlying it in greater detail than would have been possible before. The words which most obviously connect the concepts of synthesis and analysis to the schema of interrelation which has already been outlined in terms of progression and regression, and thereafter in terms of the ego's subjective and objective expansion into infinity, are these:

Der analytische Gang muss ein synthetischer seyn et vice versa - es komt nur darauf an, an welches Ende man sich stellt. Der Analytische ist durch eine Synthese, der Synthetische d[urch] eine Analyse bedingt. Die Wirkung hier, ist die Ursache dort. Der Raum ist so gross als die Zeit i.e. sie stehn in Wechseleinheit. Ewigkeit a parte post und a parte ante. Jenes analytischer, dies synthetischer Gang. Dass Synthese und Analyse in diesem Verhältnisse stehn - das ist Ich schlechthin (144, 20-27).

The term 'eternity' (*Ewigkeit*) is obviously the temporal equivalent of the spacial concept 'infinity' which was used above, and the third sentence might just as well read: infinity has the same extension as eternity, *i.e.,* they form a reciprocal unity; the German equivalent would read: Unendlichkeit ist so gross als Ewigkeit *i.e.* sie stehn in Wechseleinheit. After the ego has been defined as that point which establishes the relation of reciprocity between synthesis and analysis, its productive role as the agent, without which neither synthesis nor analysis would be, is briefly stated:

/Ich ist blos der höchstmöglichste Ausdruck für die Entstehung der Analyse und Synthese im Unbekannten. /Das Unbekannte ist das heilige Nichts für uns./ (144, 28-30)

Here, too, views previously mentioned are encountered again. The absolute sphere with respect to which the empirical ego constitutes the mutual point of origin for the synthetic and analytic approaches to infinity is a negative value, 'das heilige Nichts'.

If each direction is examined separately as a self-contained whole, then the synthetic impetus of the external or 'natural' realm can derive its point of origin, that is the beginning of the synthetic progression into infinity, only by way of an absolute analysis which is what is meant by: "< Die Natur muss über Gott zur Person steigen . . .>" (157, 5). The analytic impetus of the inner or 'personal' realm, on the other hand, derives the absolute synthesis, its prerequisite, by locating that point which is simultaneously the final term of the analysis and thus the initial term of the synthesis; this point is the zero point, so to speak, of the analytic realm and is, therefore, the person's point of tangency with nature. The quotation, the first part of which was cited above, can now be rendered in its entirety: "< Die Natur muss über Gott zur Person steigen. Die Person üb[er] d[ie] Natur zu Gott.>" (157, 5-6). Actually, these words merely state that a relative synthesis has to proceed according to absolute analysis, and that a relative analysis has to proceed according to absolute synthesis, or: the progression towards infinity in either a synthetic or analytic direction is governed by the law of absolute unity. Absolute unity predetermines the path either will traverse; absolute unity appears, therefore, as absolute analysis with respect to relative synthesis, and as absolute synthesis with respect to relative analysis. It is thus possible to explain relativity from the vantage point of either an absolute synthesis or an absolute analysis; but actually neither term is really applicable to the Absolute, since both are concepts derived from the relative. Novalis identifies himself with this latter point of view in contrast to the former two which he ascribes to Spinoza and Fichte:

Gott

Naturgott - persönlicher Gott.

Spinoza stieg bis zur Natur - Fichte bis zum Ich, oder der Person.
Ich bis zur These Gott. Gott is die Sfäre aller Analyse und
Synthese - . . .

(157, 7-11)

Novalis quite consciously insists on the undifferentiated unity of the Absolute, but since the Absolute is a negative value, not even unity, in our sense, may be predicated of it. Any statement made concerning the Absolute must be made in relative, i.e., non-absolute, terms which would mean referring to a manifestation of the Absolute rather than to the Absolute itself. If the Absolute manifests itself in the non-absolute or empirical realm, the result will be that anything predicated of the empirical is true insofar as it refers to the empirical and, at the same time, not true insofar as it refers to the Absolute; in other words, the empirical must be a paradox. Unity within a dualism, sameness of others, simultaneity of synthesis and analysis are all expressions for that exact paradox. When Novalis insists on his 'These Gott', then he will also have to insist on the essential non-difference between empirical synthesis and analysis, and, in terms of difference, on their absolute simultaneity:

Ich gehe den synthetischen und analytischen Weg zugleich - Ich betrachte jeden Schritt vor und rückwärts - (192, 26-27).

Die transscendente Natur ist zugleich immanent - so auch die immanente Person ist transscendent zugleich - und auch umgekehrt. Die Natur ist aber, wie wir gesehn haben, theils unmittelbar, theils mittelbar bedingt. Die Person gleichfalls - beyde auf verschiedene Art. Was hier unmittelbar bedingt ist, ist dort mittelbar bedingt und so vice versa. Er sind einerley Wesen - nur umgekehrt. Sie correspondiren aufs genaueste. Bildlich sind sie, wie zwey Pyramiden, die Eine Spitze haben. Sie sind wie Eine Linie. *Her* ist sie das Bild der Natur - *hin* das Bild des Ich. /Ewigkeit a parte ante et parte post. Synthetischer, analytischer Gang - *Bild überhaupt* (157, 14-26).

As we can see from Novalis' words, the loss of self-identity, which is what the term 'paradox' implies, has not only affected the empirical realm with respect to the Absolute but also the two inter-empirical constituent parts of synthetic and analytic expansion. If opposites are to be related, then their opposition has become tempered, and each has become part of the other. Synthesis and analysis are opposites, to be sure, but as was brought out before, each is dependent for its relative trend on an absolute opposition, an absolute analysis and synthesis, respectively. The Absolute, however, cannot relate to the empirical on empirical terms, even if they are absolutized; but it can and does relate the empirical on absolute terms. Relative synthesis and relative analysis, 'nature' and 'person', are absolutely related: each is the other, only in opposite directions, each is the representative of the other, each is the other's image;

and that they are that, that relation is absolute, or, as it was called in a previous quotation, "Ich schlechthin" (144, 27).

In the last fragment cited above, particularly with respect to the emphasis placed on the last two words, 'image in general' ('Bild überhaupt'), it becomes apparent that the schema of interrelation between the absolute, empirical, and inter-empirical aspects of the ego constitutes a functional relationship of a representative nature. If we reconsider Novalis' schema of interrelation as the schema of representation it actually is, we may summarize it in these words: Each member of the empirical dualism is representative of the other, and this relation as such is the manifestation of the unity of the Absolute which makes the related empirical dualism, in turn, the representative or image of the Absolute, or: "Gott hat uns nach seinem Bilde geschaffen" (141, 13) and "Gott hat den Menschen nach seinem Bilde geschaffen" (154, 11).

It must be remembered that the use of concepts like 'God' and 'Absolute' do not constitute by any means a return to pre-Kantian dogmatism on Novalis' part. These terms can just as easily be replaced by the term 'Ego', and they very often are. Even in connection with our present topic, the relation Absolute-empirical is treated with unmistakable reference to the absolute ego:

Das absolute Ich kann man auch das Absolut synthetische Ich nennen. Es ist die Synthese des Ich, inwiefern es keine eigentliche Synthese ist - jedoch zum Behuf des Analytischen Ich so genannt werden muss, weil Analyse, indem es Analyse ist, sich nur Synthese entgegensetzen kann. Diese Synthese its absolute Sfäre ohne Gränze - alle andre Synthesen sind relative Sphären i.e. Sfäre und Gränze zugleich. Sie enthält die Möglichkeit der Grenze überhaupt, im analytischen Ich. Das analytische Ich überhaupt erfüllt das Synthetische Ich. Das leztere ist die Sfäre des Analytischen - Sein Eins und Alles. Das synthetische Ich ist die nothwendige Substanz - das analytische die Mögliche und wirckliche - Ersteres in Beziehung auf jene, lezteres in Beziehung auf sich (139, 32-140, 12).

Here the relationship between the Absolute and the empirical per se is described in terms of synthesis and analysis, but, characteristically, Novalis cautions against the application of empirical names to the Absolute. What he wishes to describe is the interrelation between the ego in its dualistic, empirical, state and the ego as

absolute unity. Again the spheric image is used in order to describe the Absolute: a negative sphere, the idea of circularity ever
escaping realization. The empirical ego as its established center is
thus real ('wirckliche Substanz'), and in its direction towards the
unreachable circumference it is potentially that absolute sphere
('Mögliche Substanz'). The limitless sphere is that with respect to
which the ego-point is defined as center, the necessary point of
unity from which the different approaches to the infinite must
originate ('nothwendige Substanz').

The outline of the spherical image has appeared again, the absolute sphere with its infinite circumference and its radii extending
along an analytic and a synthetic path. This absolute sphere is the
schema of interrelation which appears throughout the "Fichte
Studies" where each dichotomy represents nothing but the two radii
of the ego's subjective and objective extensions into infinity as seen
from a different perspective. The absolute sphere is also the schema
of interrelation which we intended to expose in the second chapter,
a task which has now been completed, except, for a brief summary
of the results.

'Ego', 'Absolute', and 'God' are equivalent expressions, because
none do justice to what they all stand for; they are, just like the
term 'Absolut synthetisches Ich', projections of the absolute complement to particular aspects of the empirical realm. The Absolute
has no name: it is negative; we know of it only because the basic
dualism of subject and object which constitutes the empirical realm
lacks self-identity as a dualism insofar as its constituents lack self-
identity. Subject is not subject and object not object, synthesis is
not synthesis and analysis not analysis, but each is rather representative of the other. The point of unity, without which this reciprocity could not be, is that which we refer to as 'I'; but no matter how
closely we approach it, the 'I' by which we mean 'one' disappears
whenever we attempt to point it out and becomes a 'two', as for
instance in the dichotomy of spirit and body. Unity is manifest only
within dualism, the Absolute only within the empirical, and the
absolute unity of the ego in its simultaneous inherence within both
subject and object. If each member of the empirical dualism is
representative of the other, the dualism is as such representative of
unity, which is equivalent to saying that the empirical is represen-

tative of the Absolute. We call the empirical manifestation of Unity, the underlying unity between subject and object, between synthesis and analysis, 'I' or ego; but this unity never becomes directly apparent. Neither absolute nor empirical unity, neither absolute nor empirical ego, neither the 'absolute sphere' nor its 'center' are defined as such. They are only negatively defined by the simultaneity of the infinite progressions which we know under many names but most commonly under the names 'self' and 'nature' or 'subject' and 'object'. This is why Novalis must travel both paths simultaneously[13] in order to achieve that perfect balance which constitutes the unity of the ego, and from this vantage point the representative integration of the subjective and objective realms can be fully appreciated as they merge into one. And, by the same token, either path will lead to the other by virtue of their mutual representative relationship. Since this is so, a true understanding of either the subjective or the objective realm will invariably point to the underlying unity of which they are but manifestations, and in this sense the famous answer to the question, "Wo gehn wir denn hin?" "Immer nach Hause"[14] finds its philosophic application already in the "Fichte Studies".

It has been said in effect that Novalis envisions absolute unity to be manifest empirically in the unity of the ego which is, in turn, manifest in the reciprocal relation of the basic empirical dualism. Since this indicates an interdependence where each stands for the other and vice versa, the term 'representation' has been increasingly relied upon to convey the issues under discussion. It is now our task to examine the relevance of this concept more closely in the next chapter.

---

[13] "Ich gehe den synthetischen und analytischen Weg zugleich — Ich betrachte jeden Schritt vor und rückwärts —" (192, 26-27).
[14] Kl², I, 325.

III

REPRESENTATION: THE DYNAMICS OF THE
SCHEMA OF INTERRELATION

The concept of representation (*Repräsentation, Darstellung*) holds a pivotal position in Theodor Haering's work on Novalis, and by pointing out its importance in such an emphatic manner, he has made a most valuable contribution. This chapter, in treating the very same topic at some length, avails itself of that contribution gratefully, but with considerable reservations in matters relative to interpretation and scope of applicability.

It would be redundant to marshal detailed arguments against Theodor Haering's attempt to view Novalis' philosophical efforts as prefigurations of Hegel's system which go far beyond the limitations of Fichte's philosophy. We have already shown that Novalis' schema of interrelation between subject and object remains within the basic framework of the *Wissenschaftslehre,* and his concept of representation (*Darstellung*) will prove to be equally dependent on Fichtean thought. The concept of representation, as it appears in the "Fichte Studies", stands for the functional or dynamic aspect of the schema of interrelation which was outlined in the previous chapter. In that chapter we traced Novalis' remarkable tendency to strip everything from the Absolute to the empirical of its identity: the Absolute could be defined only in terms of the law which governs the empirical realm, and that law could only be defined in terms of the dualism it governs, that is to say, in terms of the subjective and the objective realms. Subject and object were equally elusive, since they could be defined only in terms of the absolute sphere which encompasses them. The pattern was traced; the force which surges through that pattern, and in doing so actually creates it, must however still be defined. It has already been suggested that the name of that force is 'representation' (*Darstellung*), or rather its enactment, 'representative action' (*darstellen*). Let us now add significance to that name, the significance Novalis attaches to it.

A. THE CONCEPT OF LIMITATION AND THE UNIFYING FUNCTION OF THE IMAGINATION

The theme fundamental to the idea of representation is that of 'identity' (*Identität*), which is also the initial question dealt with by both Novalis and Fichte, in the "Fichte Studies" (104 ff.) and the *Wissenschaftslehre,* respectively. In his treatment of the formula of identity, A = A, there are indications that Fichtean thought is no stranger to Novalis at the time he writes these fragments. His use of terms like 'believing' (*glauben*) and 'feeling' (*fühlen*) (105, 8-13), point to a familiarity with ideas which appear much later in the *Wissenschaftslehre* (*SW*, I, 301). It would, therefore, be difficult to consider these passages as attempts to gain a foothold in Fichte's system. A more plausible conclusion would be that the author has set out on his own from the axiom of identity, as Fichte had done, in order to see where the path would lead him. A marked difference makes itself felt with respect to a significant point: the concept of 'being' which for Fichte is devoid of meaning unless applied to the ego's self-positing action[1] is used by Novalis from the very beginning in expressed opposition to such a restriction.[2] Variance on this subject is a key divergence from Fichte's position which leaves the reader to question the author's intent. Since the non-Fichtean use of the term 'being' is not restricted to one incident but actually dominates the discussion for several pages, the possibility of an unintentional mistake in interpretation can be ruled out,[3]

---

[1] "*Sich selbst setzen* und *Seyn* sind, vom Ich gebraucht, völlig gleich" (*SW*, I, 98). And further: "(kein Ding) kann etwas anderes seyn, als ein im Ich gesetztes" (p. 99).

[2] With respect to the formula of identity, A = A, this is said: "*Ist* wird als allgemeiner Gehalt, *a* als bestimmte Form aufgestellt" (104, 4-5). C.f. *Wissenschaftslehre* (*SW*, I, 93): "Es ist nicht die Frage vom *Gehalte* des Satzes, sondern bloss von seiner *Form.*" . .   . .

[3] Haering claims that Novalis' definition of 'ist' as 'Gehalt' can be overlooked as a mistake: "Ist (= die bloss formale Verbindung) wird als allgemeiner Gehalt (sozusagen als 'Stoff'), a als Form aufgestellt; hier hat offenbar eine kleine Verwechslung stattgefunden, aber der Sinn kann nicht zweifelhaft sein" (p. 157).

and it seems equally safe to assume that it is not merely a case of obstinacy.

A brief glance at the passages in question will show Novalis' emphasis on being to be quite conscious. It undoubtedly constitutes an effort to reclaim some of the positive reality lost to that realm which the *Wissenschaftslehre* circumscribes only negatively as 'limitation' (*Begrenzung*) or 'non-ego' (*Nicht-Ich*), but in doing so, Novalis never returns to a pre-Fichtean dogmatism. The next few pages will deal with the constituent elements from which Novalis' conceptualization of the epistemological ties between subject and object evolves. It will prove to be one which envisions that 'being' can be understood only as the content of knowledge, and, conversely, that knowledge can be understood only as the 'image of being' (*ein Bild des Seyns*) which he also defines as 'non-being within being' (*Nicht-seyn im Seyn*).

When we speak of identity in an object, we speak of a limit imposed on a content which far exceeds its form. In Novalis' statement of the sentence of identity (104, 4-5), 'being' is said to be the content of 'a', which can be interpreted to mean that the same may be said of 'b', 'c' and 'd'. Such an interpretation does not apply when we speak of the ego's identity with itself, since there is no 'being' other than that which is for the ego ("D[ie] Sfäre des Ich muss für uns alles umschliessen", 104, 27-28). The term 'ego' connotes, therefore, identity of form and content ("Gehalt kann in dem Satze: Ich bin Ich nicht mehr, als im blossen Begriff des Ich liegen", 104, 25-26). The question which arises at this point is: what is to be understood by the terms 'form' and 'content' in this context, and what is their relationship?

Novalis defines the ego's formative aspect as 'absolute thetical power' (*Absolutes thetisches Vermögen*, 104, 27), as the power which allows the ego in its absolute sense, *i.e.,* the Ego, to define its own sphere in complete freedom. As formative power, the Ego is unlimitable and undefined. Yet the Ego is also content which means that it has set its own limit and experiences as such its own unlimited freedom of activity as an infinite limitation reduced to limited and defined terms. In its capacity as content of its own absolute sphere, the absolute ego exists as a finite ego whose finiteness is due to what is felt to be the limiting action of an infinite non-ego.

In other words, the dichotomy of subject and object, which constitutes the empirical realm in its entirety, is the contentual aspect of the absolute ego. The concept of limitation, which is introduced on the contentual level, is a paradoxical one: it signifies simultaneity of sameness, insofar as the point of limitation is one of tangency betweeen two separate spheres, and of otherness, insofar as the point of limitation marks the instant of separation. One sphere is thus the limiter of the other, and because of the element of sameness inherent in the act of limitation, the limiter functions as limiting agent only with respect to the thing limited, and vice versa. Any limiter is for the thing limited and in terms of the thing limited only. Accordingly, Novalis attributes the function of perception to the contentual ego ("Als Selbst Gehalt kann es Gehalt erkennen", 104, 28-29). The Ego is thus simultaneously source and recipient of its own self: source, as free and self-identical action which defines its own sphere; recipient, in its contentual role as the defined sphere which perceives an unlimited realm of objects.

What has been described until now is actually a process which Novalis outlines with reference to the sentence of identity ($A = A$) in these words: "Wir verlassen das *Identische* um es darzustellen" (104, 6-7). Self-identical action is free action and has been attributed to the Ego as 'absolute thetical power'. Viewed from the perspective of 'being enacted', from the contentual or passive aspect, free unlimited action becomes defined and limited, and thus the freely self-defined sphere of the ego contains the translation of the unlimited into terms of limitation. At the same time, because of the element of 'otherness' or estrangement which accompanies limitation, this process amounts to a projection or externalization of the Ego's free unlimited self outside itself, so that it now constitutes what is experienced as infinite limitation called 'outside world' by common experience. The freedom and unlimitability necessary for the positing of the ego's sphere becomes infinite limitation for that same sphere. Thus the reality of the Ego's free action and the reality of the infinite external limitation experienced by the empirical ego are ultimately one and the same reality. The difference arises with respect to the Ego's simultaneous function as absolute source and relative recipient. The entire process initiated by the Ego's free activity is really a "leaving of the identical in order

to demonstrate it" ("Wir verlassen das *Identische* um es darzustellen", 104, 6-7) and conversely, also an act of 'externalization'
as these words describe it:

Weil das Ich ein durchgehends bestimmtes ist, so kann es den allgemeinen Gehalt nur in sich erkennen. Inwiefern es den allgemeinen
Gehalt ausser sich versezt - muss es daran glauben. Wissen, als eine
Bestimmung, kann es ihn nicht, denn sonst müsste er *in ihm* seyn. Was
ich nicht weis, aber fühle/das Ich fühlt sich selbst, als Gehalt/glaube
ich. Die Handlung des Heraussetzens muss frey seyn - aber nur mittelbar - Sie hängt von der ersten Handlung ab - die werden wir nicht gewahr, folglich fühlen wir diese, als nichtfrey (105, 8-15).

The sphere of the ego which owes its origin to the Ego's free activity
contains that same activity in terms of limitation or: the Ego's free
activity relates to itself as the infinite limitation of its contentual
self.

   The direct relationship between free activity and content, and the
relationship between thing limited and infinite limitation are both
defined as the realm of 'feeling' and 'belief' in the lines just cited.[4]
The Ego 'feels' itself as content in the act of self-consciousness; its
contentual self 'feels' its externalized free activity and 'believes' its
existence. Knowledge, in this context, is then the defined image of
the undefinable placed between free action as absolute thetical
power and free action as antithetical power. The Ego 'feels' itself
as the knower of a 'felt' unknown, and its relative sphere comprises
the limited effort to reabsorb the infinite. Being is ascribed by the
absolute thetical power to all it contains, and it contains all, since
it is absolute. The absolute ego, or absolute thetical power, is the
potential container of everything perceivable by the empirical ego
which means that it is both the all-encompassing sphere under
which the empirical ego and its object become united as well as the

---

[4] The terminology in lines 9-13, when compared to Fichte's, seems to in-
dicate a familiarity with very advanced stages of the *Wissenschaftslehre:*
"...Etwas, das lediglich durch die *Beziehung eines* Gefühls möglich wird,
ohne dass das Ich *seiner Anschauung* desselben sich bewusst wird, noch bewusst werden kann, und *das daher gefühlt zu sein scheint,* wird geglaubt. —
An Realität überhaupt, sowohl die des *Ich,* findet lediglich *ein Glaube statt"*
(*SW*, I, 301). The entry is from the latter half of the "Third Part", published
in 1795, whereas the first two parts were published in 1794.

initial act by which the division into empirical ego and objects takes place. Novalis ends this particular speculation on identity with the telling parallelism:

> *Theilen* und *vereinen*
> Reines und empirisches Ich   (105, 20-21)

After the preconditions for knowledge have been outlined in this fashion, it is now possible to determine the concept of knowledge itself within this framework as constituting a representative relationship which Novalis calls image (*Bild*):

> Was für eine Beziehung ist das Wissen? Es ist ein Seyn ausser dem Seyn, das doch im Seyn ist. /Theilen - vereinen/ Das Bewusstseyn ist ein Seyn ausser dem Seyn im Seyn. Was ist aber das? Das Ausser dem Seyn muss kein rechtes Seyn seyn. Ein unrechtes Seyn ausser dem Seyn ist ein Bild - Also muss jenes ausser dem Seyn ein Bild des Seyns im Seyn seyn. D[as] Bewusstseyn ist folglich ein Bild des Seyns im Seyn. Nähere Erklärung des Bildes. /Zeichen/ Theorie des Zeichens. /Theorie der Darstellung oder des Nichtseyns im Seyn, um das Seyn für sich *auf gewisse Weise da* seyn zu lassen/ Theorie des Raums und der Zeit beym Bilde (106, 1-13).

In more specific terms, that which common experience calls consciousness of objects is here called 'a being outside of being within being' ("Das Bewusstseyn ist ein Seyn ausser dem Seyn im Seyn", 106, 4). This terminology attempts to convey the paradoxical quality of any representative function which simultaneously is and is not that which it represents. In like fashion, the defined sphere of human knowledge is one with the objects it contains, yet it is at the same time different from them. The difference between object and knowledge stems from the identity of knowledge and knower. If we return for a moment to the formula of identity, then A = A means that A leaves its objective identity in order to assume 'non-identical' being within our sphere of knowledge ("Wir verlassen das *Identische* um es darzustellen — ... wir stellen es durch sein Nichtseyn, durch ein Nichtidentisches vor — Zeichen", 104, 6-11). This is accomplished by the initial, or objective, A's becoming the uniform determinant of the A within that sphere ("Zeichen — ein bestimmtes für ein gleichförmig bestimmendes", 104, 11-12) along with the equal determining power of the Ego which determines the sphere as such ("dieses gleichförmig bestimmende muss eigentlich durchaus unmittelbar das mitgetheilte Zeichen durch eben die Bewegung bestimmen, wie ich — Frey und doch so wie ich", 104, 12-14).

Fichte traces man's ability to perceive an object as self-identical, and therefore as one, to the self-identity of the beholder. Novalis accepts Fichte's manner of argument and proceeds, in direct imitation of it, from the analysis of A = A (104, 1-21) to the investigation of the implications expressed in the sentence, "I am I": "Anwendung des bereits gesagten auf den Satz: Ich bin Ich. Grammaticalisch enthält er dreyfach idem. Gehalt kann in dem Satze: Ich bin Ich nicht mehr, als im blossen Begriff des Ich liegen" (104, 22-26). The self-identical I, absolute thetical power, all inclusive sphere ("Was ist Ich?/Absolutes thetisches Vermögen/D[ie] Sfäre des Ich muss für uns alles umschliessen", 104, 27-28), "leaves its identity" insofar as it becomes a perceiver (the object left its identity insofar as it was perceived). It is thus no longer thetical power but content (the Ego is conscious of its own self as 'subject' of 'objects', or: "Als Selbst Gehalt kann es Gehalt erkennen", 104, 28-29). Its function as perceiver is to give form to everything for the Ego, and it exists as content for the Ego only in that function ("Das Erkennen deutet auf sein *Ich*seyn", 104, 29). It determines its content and is, as this determinant, content for the Ego. The perceiver's link with the Ego is his power of determination, a power which can only have been derived from the Ego; as content, the ego is therefore determined by nothing but its own self which simply means that it accepts the objects which become its content for no other reason but that it is receptive to them, *i.e.*: that it accepts them ("Als Grund alles Bestimmens für d[as] Ich, oder aller *Form* ist es mithin Grund seiner eignen Bestimmung, oder Form. Kürzer: es ist eine selbständige Bestimmung des Gehalts — damit hat es *sich* selbst *alle* Bestimmung gegeben. Spontaneität seiner Bestimmung — Es nimmt z.B. A an, weil es a annimmt", 104, 29-105, 2).

In order to enter the sphere of non-identity, the self-identical ego has to divide itself into perceiver and the externalized object of perception; or, in more Fichtean terms, the infinite activity of the ego limits itself which means nothing else but that the sphere of the ego is defined by infinite limitation.

Novalis' analysis of the sentence of identity leads, in summary, to the following position: Identity entails a process of mutual representation between infinity and limitation, a process which causes the Ego to exist as both infinite action and finite sphere, and the object as both infinite limitation and finite image. It is obvious that the dual relation of infinity to the finite, on the Ego's level and on the object's level, respectively, presents the absolute concept of unity or identity from an empirical perspective. The Absolute is one, and its breakdown into polar categories like 'infinite' and 'finite' already belongs to the empirical realm, to the realm which is representative of the Absolute. The pattern Novalis traces as the mutually representative process between the infinite and the finite is a familiar one. It has been introduced in the previous chapter as Novalis' schema of interrelation where the empirical aspect of the Ego proved to be a subjective and an objective relation to infinity in the order of an analysis and of a synthesis. At the time, it was not necessary to explain by what power the fusion between the finite and the infinite takes place; our present discussion, however, has led directly to a point at which such an explanation is required.

Fichte's analysis of the sentence of identity leads to the very same point where the interrelation between the infinite and the finite, the unlimited and the limited, has to be discussed. From these speculations he derives his concept of the 'power of the imagination' (*Einbildungskraft*). We shall now briefly examine Fichte's arguments and compare his resultant definition of imagination to the one Novalis furnishes.

". . . keine Unendlichkeit, keine Begrenzung; keine Begrenzung, keine Unendlichkeit":[5] this is the key relationship underlying the entire discussion which, in its final stages, leads to the concept of imagination. Upon closer examination of this formula, its smooth interdependency as well as the identity of the respective terms 'limitation' and 'infinity' do not seem as evident as could have been expected.

If one begins with the first statement, "keine Unendlichkeit, keine Begrenzung", the following concept of limitation evolves: Limitation can be effected by no complete 'other', since that would exclude the point of contact or tangency necessary to the act of limitation. Limitation can be effected only by a 'same', and is therefore 'self-limitation'. By the same reason the realm of the 'same' is unaffectable by an 'other', because no possible relationship can exist between the two. The 'same' is thus unlimitable and in that sense unlimited or infinite.

Infinity inheres, therefore, within the limited, and it does so in the aspect of self-identity which is in turn equivalent to the self-limitation. Yet, limitation includes the aspect of 'otherness' which can also be defined as non-identity or the negative circumscription of the self-identical. Insofar as the stress within the self-identical is on the 'limit' rather than 'self', the 'other' becomes the limiter and as such is now empowered as was the limited in its aspect of sameness before. The power of limitation, and along with that infinity, are now the limiter's; however, as limiter it is no longer simply and absolutely self-identical but it is rather directly dependent on the thing limited. The limiter's function is to limit and only in this derived sense is it what it is.

Limiter and limited are thus exactly the same with respect to the aspect of infinitiy; they differ with respect to their actions: the action of the limited is simple, spontaneous, and non-directed ($=$ simple self-identity: $A = A$), and the action of the limiter is also spontaneous, but its direction is determined by the object of limitation (just as $-A = -A$, which is dependent on A for its very terms).

The second statement, "keine Begrenzung, keine Unendlichkeit", is the obvious reference to the sort of infinity derived from examining the 'other' aspect of limitation. 'Unendlichkeit' assumes a meaning directly dependent on the respective framework within which it is used, and must not be understood as independently invariable. 'Begrenzung' is an equally elusive term, unless its dual aspect of sameness and otherness is taken into consideration. Within either framework the concept of limitation will be of a different significance as was the case with the concept of infinity.

One more question to be investigated here concerns the mutual interdependency of the two statements. It is easily determined that limit is directly dependent on infinity, if it is to be considered under the aspect of 'sameness' it entails. The difficulty arises once infinity is to be considered dependent on limitation, since the infinite simply does not contain the need for limitation. Precisely the creation of this need for limitation is attributable to what Fichte calls an *Anstoss*. This term contains really no solution to the problem; it is actually nothing but an acknowledgment of it. As such, the term is by no means dismissible as meaningless. On the contrary, the most appropriate reference to the action of the infinite from the vantage point of limitation would have to be in terms of the completed act and thus the fact of limitation is viewed as a task still to be accomplished. The setting of this task of limitation is not essential to infinity per se, and constitutes in its spontaneity something foreign to it. It constitutes an *Anstoss*. Limit is actually essential to infinity because of the accomplished fact of limitation, and only in that light can the statement "keine Begrenzung, keine Unendlichkeit" be understood.

The Ego, because this is what has been under discussion all along, is thus infinite positing action as well as limited posited self, and as the latter it acts as recipient of its unlimited action which is experienced as limitation by an infinite action from without.

The limited ego in its limited state can receive the infinite limiting action only on limited terms (manner of identity between subject and object), yet as unlimited action it has to be posited outside the ego's now limited realm (= the 'other' aspect of the object).

Our every moment of experience is a paradox because the object can be identical with the self insofar as it is contained within consciousness, yet at the same time, it is an 'other', entirely foreign to the self. The basis of this paradox has just been shown: it is no other than the ego's positing of its self as finite and infinite. The power of imagination (*Einbildungskraft*) is, in Fichte's own words, the point of unity through which the oscillations between finite and infinite course,[6] and our everyday experience attests to the same

---

[6] "Dieser Wechsel des Ich in und mit sich selbst, da es sich endlich und unendlich zugleich setzt — ein Wechsel, der gleichsam in einem Widerstreite mit sich selbst besteht, und dadurch sich selbst reproducirt, indem das Ich unvereinbares vereinigen will, jetzt das unendliche in die Form des endlichen aufzunehmen versucht, jetzt, zurückgetrieben, es wieder ausser derselben setzt, und in dem nemlichen Momente abermals es in die Form der Endlichkeit aufzunehmen versucht — ist das Vermögen der *Einbildungskraft*" (*SW*, I, 215).

function of that power whenever the image of an object appears to us.

Fichte's concept of imagination refers essentially to the power which tends to reestablish absolute unity according to the law which the prime act of self-limitation has established. Novalis' point of view is the same, except that his interpretation applies in particular to his schema of interrelation. It was mentioned before that the Ego's free and absolute action defines its own sphere, and that for this self-enacted sphere the Ego's absolute activity becomes an external act of limitation. Absolute action is thus, from the contentual or empirical perspective an act of externalization. Or, rather, the prime act decrees the law by which the limited ego relates to its limiter, that is to say, the law by which subject and object relate:

Die Handlung des Heraussetzens muss frey seyn - aber nur mittelbar - Sie hängt von der ersten Handlung ab - die werden wir nicht gewahr, folglich fühlen wir diese, als nichtfrey. Warum wir sie nicht gewahr werden - weil sie das Gewahrwerden erst möglich macht, und folglich dis *in* ihrer Sfäre liegt - die Handlung des Gewahrwerdens kann ja also nicht aus ihrer Sfäre herausgehn und die Muttersfäre mitfassen wollen. *Theilen* und *vereinen*. Reines und empirisches Ich (105, 13-21).

From the perspective of the empirical ego the absolute act of division is reperformed as an act of unification ("*Theilen* und *vereinen*. Reines und empirisches Ich*", 105, 20-21). The power by which this fusion is accomplished is called imagination (*Einbildungskraft*): "Die Einbildungskraft ist das verbindende Mittelglied — die Synthese — die *Wechselkraft*", (186, 10-11). Novalis also defines imagination, in terms of his spheric schema of interrelation, as the power which brings the binary progression into infinity to a halt at any given point so that the never-realized infinite sphere of absolute unity assumes an ever-present representative reality:

Die Zirkellinie kan überall unterbrochen - die Pole der Ansch[auung] und Vorstellung überall ge- und versezt werden. Die Einbild[ungs] Kr[aft] äussert sich, als Einfalls oder Hemmkraft. A[nschauung] und V[orstellung] sind, für sich genommen, stätig. Ihre Unterbrechung giebt ihnen erst Realität - insofern nemlich Realität aus der identischen Mischung von Ansch[auung] und Vorstell[ung] besteht (190, 19-25).

Within the framework of Novalis' schema of interrelation, the power of the imagination is the force which attempts to fill the absolute ego's sphere from an empirical center and in so doing establishes the image of that sphere at each and every point.

Novalis' concept of the imagination furnishes a new perspective from which his ideas on 'being', 'knowledge', 'sign', and 'image', presented of necessity in a rudimentary and incomplete fashion up to this point in the present chapter, must be reexamined. The concept of the imagination is also the vantage point from which the ego's binary extension into infinity will appear as thought perception (*Vorstellung*) and sense perception (*Anschauung*). Even though these terms had to be employed previously, their true significance within the context of Novalis' thought can be appreciated only now. We shall begin by reinterpreting[7] two passages from the "Fichte Studies" after which an analysis of the concepts of thought perception and sense perception will conclude the first section of the present chapter:

Das Bewusstseyn ist ein Seyn ausser dem Seyn im Seyn. Was ist aber das? Das Ausser dem Seyn muss kein rechtes Seyn seyn. Ein unrechtes Seyn ausser dem Seyn ist ein Bild - Also muss jenes ausser dem Seyn ein Bild des Seyns im Seyn seyn. D[as] Bewusstseyn ist folglich ein Bild des Seyns im Seyn. Nähere Erklärung des Bildes. /Zeichen/ Theorie des Zeichens. / Theorie der Darstellung oder des Nichtseyns im Seyn, um das Seyn für sich *auf gewisse Weise* da seyn zu lassen/ . . . (106, 4-12)

In connection with the word "Zeichen", also these lines should be added:

. . . wir stellen es [das Identische][8] durch sein Nichtseyn, durch ein Nichtidentisches vor - Zeichen - ein bestimmtes für ein gleichförmig bestimmendes - dieses gleichförmig bestimmende muss eigentlich durchaus unmittelbar das mitgetheilte Zeichen durch eben die Bewegungen bestimmen, wie ich - (104, 10-14).

'Non-being', 'image', 'outside of being', and 'consciousness' are

---

[7]   The quotations from Kl², II, 106, 1-13 and Kl², II, 104, 10-14 have already been cited, at least in part, on pp. 66-67 of this chapter.
[8]   My insert.

synonymous in this passage which, as has been pointed out before, constitutes a negative evaluation of that realm of knowledge. As a positive value, 'being' stands juxtaposed to it as both that which the image depicts and that for whom the image is. Being as depicted in the mind is there only insofar as its beholder is itself again nothing else but that very being.[9] If 'being' and 'beholder' are one and the same, how is it possible to attain the element of 'otherness' necessary to the concept of image or representation? Insofar as the ego is the object of its own consciousness, it is, and insofar as it is its own object, it functions as subject for an objectivity believed to be external to it; this, its relation to itself as object, a relation other than the one it has to its externalized objects, is that necessary element of difference.

Knowledge of a particular object involves differentiation which entails a common ground as well as differing characteristics. Insofar as the object is objective, it stands for that which is common to all objects; insofar as it is this particular object, it introduces an additional aspect other than its common one. The relative ground in the objective sphere is essential objectivity per se, whereas the differentiating ground comprises that which is referred to as individual characteristics or 'accidentals'. The same dichotomy exists in the subjective realm; here the common ground is furnished by the object's inherence within the subject, and the differentiating ground is its otherness as thing. This could also be stated in the following manner: The *an sich* and *für mich* characteristics of anything known furnish the common and the differentiating ground from the objective perspective in that order and do the same in reverse order from the subjective perspective.

The prime determinant for anything representative is that which it represents; the secondary determinant is that which effects the difference between thing representing and thing represented. In the present definition of representation, it seems obvious that the prime determinant is 'being' whereas the secondary one is the ego as ego. It appears to be a thoroughly dogmatic position, were it not for the very fact that representation or imagery is actually the topic dis-

---

[9] Or as it is expressed by Novalis: "Als selbst Gehalt kann es [das Ich] Gehalt erkennen" (104, 28-29).

cussed. 'Being' as such has been completely removed from the sphere of knowledge[10] and can be dealt with in terms of its image only. If one recalls that Fichte talks of the world of objects as ego-limitation only, that is to say, only in terms of the ego and never in terms of the limiter as an entity in itself, then representation within this context means the exact same thing with the emphasis on the limited state of the ego rather than on its freedom. In other words, the power of imagination (*Einbildungskraft*) unites the limited and the free aspects of the ego in an image (*Bild*).[11]

The term 'sign' (*Zeichen*) has been mentioned in connection with representation ("Zeichen / Theorie des Zeichens. / Theorie der Darstellung . . .", 106, 10-11). It differs from an image, at least with respect to the passages presently under consideration, insofar as the determinative function of the ego is more accentuated in a sign. The represented object "A" which the ego beholds is not only an image but also a sign, because it is FOR the ego, and thus determined by it; this is what is meant by: ". . . dieses Gleichförmig bestimmende muss eigentlich durchaus unmittelbar das mitgetheilte Zeichen durch eben die Bewegung bestimmen, wie ich — . . ." (104, 11-13). The consideration of the concepts sign and image opens an area of additional concepts like thought perception (*Vorstellung*) and sense perception (*Anschauung*) which will serve to explain the relation between sign and image on a more specific basis.

The ego's dual nature appears to its own experience as reality divided into a sensual and rational realm. Yet both are united, and that point of unity is what is actually meant by the term 'empirical ego'. Its inclination toward one or the other is called *Anschauung* in the former case, and *Vorstellung* in the latter. The power which brings about their interrelation, and is thus the active expanding circumference of unity, is the power of imagination. In this sense, *Anschauung* is imagination as applied to the sensual realm, and *Vorstellung* is imagination as applied to the rational one: "Das Sub-

---

[10]   C.f. pp. 65-66 above: discussion on *glauben* and *fühlen*.
[11]   "Wie kann d[as] empirische Ich sein *eignes Bild* entwerfen, ohne ein objectives Medium anzunehmen. /Eintheilung der Einbildungskraft./ Sinnlichkeit und Verstand correspondiren aufs genaueste — weil sie Eins im Dritten sind" (169, 29-32).

ject, welches als Vorstellung Ich heisst, ist eine ruhende Kraft, ein Festes, Einfaches, Veränderndes, ohne sich zu verändern. Anschauung und Vorstellung ist Eins. Jene Beziehung der Einbild[ungs] Kr[aft] auf die Sinnlichkeit — diese Beziehung d[er] Einb[ildungs] Kr[aft] auf d[en] Verstand" (168, 23-27). By the power of the imagination the ego establishes itself in the sensual realm as permanent reference point which enables it to lend pertinent unity to a realm which is essentially its utter negation. The establishment of the ego as a physical entity 'creates' the material which reason will thereafter mold according to its laws. The molded product, generally known as 'object', as well as the ego, in its capacity of reference point, are both products of the same power, the power of imagination:

Einbild[ungs] Kr[aft] besteht aus Sinnlichkeit und Verstand - beyde müssen vereinigt schaffende und bildende Kraft seyn. Sie können nicht die Vorstellung der Einbildungskraft bestimmen - die Einbild[ungs] Kr[aft] muss ihre Vorstellungen bestimmen (169, 9-13).

Also in this context, the topic of the previous chapter is illustrated once more insofar as the relative function of 'one' as reference point for unity, relative to its infinite divisibility, and as reference point for infinite multiplicity, relative to its infinite multiplicability is demonstrated in these words: "Das Vorstellungsvermögen enthält das Einfache der Form, und d[as] Mannichfache des Stoffs - d[as] Anschauungsverm[ögen] das Einfache des Stoffs und d[as] Mannichfache der Form" (170, 15-17).

Now a position has been reached where it is possible to establish a definition of image and sign in the terms just outlined:

/ Bild ist eine vorgestellte Anschauung. Zeichen eine angeschaute Vorstellung./ Symbolische Bildungskraft. Imagination./ (171, 16-18)

And in the spirit of the previous chapter, the quotation continues:

Was ist Vorstellung und Anschauung?/ Es giebt keine absolute Form, und keinen absoluten Stoff. Sie bedingen sich alle wechselweise im Kreise./ (171, 19-21)

Language is the concept most obviously connected with signification, so that Novalis feels justified in equating language and sign a few fragments later:

Zeichen - Bild. Im Zeichen praevalirt der Begriff - im Bild die Anschauung - Sprach oder Begriffbild (188, 18-19).

In another fragment, language and the very process of substitution, the process of having one object represent another, is clearly outlined within this framework:

Sprache: Verknüpfung des besondern sinnlichen Gedankenstoffs mit sinnlichen Zeichen. Zeichen ist eine hypothetische Anschauung, bedingt durch eine Vorstellung (189, 1-3).

Let us now return briefly to the words already cited, "/Bild ist eine vorgestellte Anschauung. Zeichen eine angeschaute Vorstellung./" and see them reappear with a telling variation: "Vorgestellte Anschauung, und angeschaute Vorstellung machen also das Wesen der Einbildungskraft aus" (177, 25-26).

In order to do full justice to these words, they must be quoted within their more immediate context. This will show the present topic to include important ideas on freedom, philosophy, and beauty, ideas which, in part, refer to thoughts already made familiar in the initial part of this chapter. At the same time, a new variation on the theme of representation, the nature of aesthetics, is introduced. The following subdivision of this chapter will, therefore, begin with a quotation of the entire section of fragment number 234 (177, 12-26) which contains the passage in question, and the discussion thereafter will be devoted to a detailed exposition of its significance.

B.   TRUTH AND BEAUTY AS LAWS OF THE IMAGINATION

/Eine Art von Wechselbestimmungssatz, ein reines Associationsgesetz scheint mir der oberste Grundsatz seyn zu müssen - ein hypothetischer Satz./[12]

---

[12]   The term 'hypothetical' does not apply here in a Kantian sense. This becomes apparent in its use in general, and more specifically in its identification with 'reciprocity', the category associated with 'disjunctive judgment' and not with 'hypothetical judgment'.

Allgemeingültige Filosofie würde die *Fixirung* der sogenannten Subjectivität, also ein *freyes* Factum, oder die Annahme eines hypothetischen, freyen Satzes, voraussetzen. Man kann so gewiss seine Filosofie wahr nennen - so gewiss man etwas schön nennt. Die reinste Vorstellung ist Anschauung - die reine Anschauung - Vorstellung. Das
reinste Subjective ist objectiv - Das reine Objective - subjectiv. / Princip
der Schönheit - begründet die Vorstellung und Anschauung. / In der
Anschauung müssen wir beym Gange vom Besondern zum Allgemeinen, auf die Vorstellung - In der Vorstellung - auf die Anschauung
gerathen.

/ Vorgestellte Anschauung, und angeschaute Vorstellung machen also
das Wesen der Einbildungskraft aus./ (177, 12-26)

/ Freyheit bezeichnet den Zustand der *schwebenden* Einbild[ungs]
Kr[aft]. / Gesetz muss Produkt der *Freyheit* seyn/

Wir denken und schaun immer nur *Product* an. Aller Transitus - alle
Bewegung ist Wircksamkeit der Einbild[ungs] Kr[aft] (188, 20-25).

These words constitute a summary of all that has been said up to
this point. The highest axiom of absolute unity necessary to the
establishment of the point of relative unity between two spheres
thus made reciprocal was central to the previous chapter, and finds
its reaffirmation here in its essential relevance to the present topic
of representation. This axiomatic law of absolute unity is executed
by the power of imagination which reunites without cessation sense
perception (*Anschauung*) and rational perception (*Vorstellung*),
the dual spheres of the empirical ego. The general authority inherent in such an axiom could never be dependent on the accidence
of empirical data, and must, therefore, be an element of the subjective realm. Since it is the fundamental axiom, the ultimate and
basic law, it is the axiom of subjectivity itself, thus necessarily de-
claring the subject to be absolute and free.[13] As the science of

---

[13]   This deification of the subject must not be misunderstood as absolutizing
the relative, empirical ego. Before Hume's skepticism, the same process
applied to the non-subjective realm resulted in the postulating of an extra-
subjective deity which did by no means imply that any one object or sum of
objects was declared absolute. Both medieval metaphysics and a system like
Spinoza's make any such confusion impossible. The former was guarded
against it by a never-ceasing watchfulness against pantheism, thus empha-
sizing the gulf between the divine and creation; the latter, although pan-

science, the knowledge of knowledge, philosophy would require such an axiom both as its prerequisite and as its potential conclusion, and the only ascertainable aspect of either is the philosophic process itself. For this reason Fichte finds himself involved in an essentially circular argument where he seemingly presupposes the conclusion. He comments repeatedly on his 'circles' in an attempt to convince the reader that this manner of argument is not only essential to his position but even a guide to its correctness. The very concept *Tathandlung* is nothing but an expression of this necessary circularity, since it simply states that the result of the action must needs antecede the action itself.[14] It is in this spirit that Novalis can equate 'truth' and 'beauty' by saying that one can call one's philosophy true with the same certainty with which one applies the standard of beauty. ("Man kann so gewiss seine Filosofie wahr nennen — so gewiss man etwas schön nennt", 177, 17-18). Kant's definition of aesthetic pleasure as 'disinterested pleasure' (*uninteressiertes Wohlgefallen*),[15] his elimination of objective purposefulness from the aesthetic, has made it possible to view art as a realm wherein the object has existence only as the bearer and transmittor of the subjective. The general criterion which removes aesthetics from the stigma of pure relativism can, obviously, not be objective in the light of this definition, and must, therefore, con-

---

theistic, separates man, and thus the realm accessible to him, drastically from the divine by placing no restriction on God whereas His creature is confined to thought and extension. The same division must occur when the subjective realm assumes the function formerly held by the external or objective realm. It does occur insofar as one speaks of 'pure' or 'absolute ego' and 'empirical ego' or 'subject'.

[14] This view is not entirely new to Western thought; Aristotle's 'final cause' describes a similar necessity.

[15] The entire section of the *Critique of Judgment* which is entitled "Analysis of the Concept of Beauty" ("Analytik des Schönen") deals with aesthetic pleasure as one which is disengaged from the objective realm on either a sensual or a rational basis: "Man kann sagen: dass unter allen diesen drei Arten des Wohlgefallens, das des Geschmacks am Schönen einzig und allein ein uninteressiertes und freies Wohlgefallen sei; denn kein Interesse, weder das der Sinne, noch das der Vernunft, zwingt den Beifall ab" (V, 278). Kant goes on to define beauty with this sentence on page 279: "Geschmack ist das Beurteilungsvermögen eines Gegenstandes oder einer Vorstellungsart durch ein Wohlgefallen, oder Missfallen, ohne alles Interesse. Der Gegenstand eines solchen Wohlgefallens heisst schön."

stitute part of each subject. It is, then, subjectivity per se which is reflected in the aesthetic object; or, in other words, the aesthetic object functions as a mirror of subjectivity per se, and aesthetic pleasure is self-recognition in an 'other'. Aesthetic law or standard inheres in the subject and precedes the work of art, but the manifestation of this law becomes apparent to the individual subject only through the individual art-object.

Philosophy is concerned with truth. If all there is can be thought of only as 'for' the ego, so that the sphere of subjectivity is all-encompassing, then all of philosophy's observations will be relegated to that sphere, and they will progress according to the ultimate law of subjectivity which is both their beginning and end. The ego proclaims something as true insofar as it functions both as source and recipient of the law per se, and the focal reflector in this instance is the empirical ego as the uniform point of reference for the subjective and the objective realms. Truth and beauty are both standards of subjectivity or, in Fichtean terms, of the absolute ego, reflected in the relative subject and in the object, respectively.

Analogy relative to mathematical truth, as Kant and his contemporaries understood it, may be helpful in envisioning how the above is to be understood. The certainty of truth inherent in geometrical axioms is derived from the fact that geometrical figures are constructed according to laws which are inherent to the mind of the person who constructs them. This is the reason why the properties of triangles, for instance, will apply with absolute certainty to the infinite totality of triangles per se. Even though it would be quite impossible for anyone to test this claim empirically, there is no doubt as to its veracity. Thus, here too the same circularity applies: a particular action, *i.e.*, the construction of a triangle, is preceded by its result in the form of a general subjective law, and the triangle, too, is mirror of a standardized subjectivity; or, in the language of the *Critique of Pure Reason:*

Dem ersten, der den gleichschenkligen Triangel demonstrierte (er mag nun THALES oder wie man will geheissen haben), dem ging ein Licht auf; denn er fand, dass er nicht dem, was er in der Figur sahe, oder auch dem blossen Begriffe derselben nachspüren und gleichsam davon ihre Eigenschaften ablernen, sondern durch das, was er nach den Begriffen

selbst a priori hineindachte und darstellete (durch Konstruktion), hervorbringen müsse, und dass er, um sicher etwas a priori zu wissen, der
Sache nichts beilegen müsse, als was aus dem notwendig folgte, was er
seinem Begriffe gemäss selbst in sie gelegt hat (III, 15).

In the passage cited at the beginning of this section, Novalis also envisions a purely subjective criterion for truth; he, however, does not
speak of merely object-directed, empirical truth, as is the case with
Kant when he establishes space, time, and categories as criteria
for sense perception (*Anschauung*) and thought perception (*Vorstellung*). Novalis speaks of the criterion for truth per se, the criterion for thought on thought, for philosophy, for the envisionment
of the human situation as such ("Allgemeingültige Filosofie würde
die *Fixirung* der sogenannten Subjectivität, also ein *freyes* Factum,
oder die Annahme eines hypothetischen, freyen Satzes, voraussetzen", 177, 15-17). Essentially, this conceptualization places the
criterion for objectivity per se into the subject. Fichte does exactly
this in his first axiom (*Grundsatz*) of the *Wissenschaftslehre* where
he establishes the self-identity and freedom of the ego as a prerequisite for the identity of any object perceived;[16] the first axiom,
in turn, furnishes the necessary element of unity for the third axiom
of reciprocal limitation between relative subject and object. The
basic maxims of the *Wissenschaftslehre* meet Novalis' demands for
a 'pure law of association as prime axiom' ("... ein reines Associationsgesetz scheint mir der oberste Grundsatz seyn zu müssen —
ein hypothetischer Satz", 177, 12-14). It is this law of free association which establishes for Novalis the criterion not only of truth
but of beauty as well ("Man kann so gewiss seine Filosofie wahr
nennen — so gewiss man etwas schön nennt", 177, 17-18).

The elimination of the objective realm as an independent force
reduces objectivity to a state of self-estrangement produced by an
alienating and unifying momentum. In short, objectivity is repre-

---

[16]   "Soll der Satz: A = A (oder bestimmter, das jenige was in ihm schlechthin gesetzt ist = X) gewiss seyn, so muss auch der Satz: Ich bin, gewiss seyn.
Nun ist est Thatsache des empirischen Bewusstseyns, dass wir genöthigt sind,
X für schlechthin gewiss zu halten; mithin auch den Satz: Ich bin — auf
welchen X sich gründet. Es ist demnach Erklärungsgrund aller Thatsachen
des empirischen Bewusstseyns, dass vor allem Setzen im Ich vorher das Ich
selbst gesetzt sey. —" (*SW*, I, 25).

sentative of absolute unity; it represents self-identical and free unity which functions as both source and end. Objectivity is representation per se, and it covers the realm commonly referred to as subject and object, the entire scope of the empirical. Since it is nothing but representation, it cannot show anything but absolute unity in its dual aspect. The difference between absolute and empirical is attributable to a mere shift in perspective. Where absolute unity functions as both source and end, relative unity, as was outlined in the previous chapter, constitutes the mutual point of origin for a dual approach to the infinite. Infinity, in turn, is nothing else but absolute unity viewed from a relative perspective. Also, the two approaches themselves owe their difference to nothing but the same difference established between empirical and absolute. In the external realm, the relative point of unity[17] is the ego limited by, and as such part of, the infinite totality of its physical environment. This physical environment is in turn represented as image in the ego's mind. In the internal realm unity is totality[18] insofar as the ego serves as uniform receptacle for the infinitely expandable content derived from the external realm. In this case, the content is, in its ordered coherence, representative of the ego's unifying power. If it were not for this power, the ego would be entirely submerged in the external realm; it would lose its identity, and with it limitation as limitation, *i.e.*, the external realm, would cease to exist. External objectivity exists for the subject which means it exists merely as potential content of the subject, or: "Das reine Objective —" [ist] "subjectiv./" (177, 20-21).

Sense perception (*Anschauung*) is actually nothing else but an extension from the particular, from the ego as relative point of unity, to the general. The general gains its coherence only in being limited by the projection of a relative totality, and relative totality is the characteristic of thought perception. Novalis refers to this manner of progression from the particular to the general as: "In der Anschauung müssen wir beym Gange vom Besondern zum Allgemeinen, auf die Vorstellung —... gerathen" (177, 22-24). Thought perception in the pure sense is, in its turn, nothing else but the

---

[17]   This point is representative of relativity per se.
[18]   This totality is representative of totality per se or of absolute unity.

potential totality of sense perception in the reverse direction, from the general to the specific: "Das reinste Subjective ist objectiv —... In der Vorstellung —" [müssen wir beym Gange vom Allgemeinen zum Besondern] "auf die Anschauung gerathen" (177, 20-24). The terms subjective and objective actually describe nothing else but unity in its dual aspect of part and totality, and the reciprocal directions, from totality to part and from part to totality, respectively, which this dualism makes possible. The mutual point of departures, the center, for these opposite directions is the empirical ego with its unifying power of imagination ("Vorgestellte Anschauung, und angeschaute Vorstellung machen also das Wesen der Einbildungskraft aus./" 177, 25-26). The establishing of such a central point in its capacity as central point is only possible with respect to an absolute sphere. Since it does not exist as final sphere either as antecedent or result of the empirical ego, it can only be understood negatively in the sense negative theology understands God 'negatively'. This is the reason why Novalis says that only 'products' are ascertainable, never freedom, *i.e.*, the producer itself ("/Gesetz muss Produkt der *Freyheit* seyn / Wir denken und schaun immer nur *Product* an", 188, 22-23). The absolute subject is understood as pure freedom, or pure action, since it establishes the empirical ego and constitutes the infinity in which both directions go.

Beauty is the law of imagination, the principle of both sense and thought perceptions, Novalis states, and with that, he characterizes beauty as the principle of absolute unity manifest in the direct relation between OBJECT AND SUBJECT; its basic realm is that of sense perception, and 'image' (*Bild*) is its delegate to thought perception. Philosophic truth, which was discussed earlier within this context, is also nothing else but a principle of that same absolute unity manifest in the relation between SUBJECT AND OBJECT; its basic realm is that of thought perception, and 'sign' (*Zeichen*), 'language' (*Sprache*), or 'word' (*Wort*) is its delegate to sense perception.

Both beauty and truth are one and the same law. They constitute the law of the imagination, the law of the empirical ego's dynamic aspect, according to which the moments of subjectivity and objectivity relate to one another. When the momentum of the relationship appears to move from the 'outer world' to the 'inner world', the resultant image will have been effected according to the criterion of beauty. When the momentum appears to move in the opposite direction, any resultant significance will have been effected according to the criterion of truth. In other words, man perceives his environment according to the free criterion of beauty, and he affects it according to the free criterion of truth. Ugliness and lack of truth appear in direct proportion to the inhibitions man feels to have been placed on the free exercise of this criterion. Beauty and truth are terms which refer from the dualistic perspective of the empirical realm to the one, freely enacted, law of association between subject and object, just as the terms subject and object refer, from the same perspective, to the basic unity of the empirical ego. If the unity of the ego were to be restated empirically as unity, it would have to be done by the power of the same law according to which the empirical dualism is related. Since the law of association is manifest empirically as beauty and truth, a complete fusion of those two manifestations in an empirical act would most appropriately restate the ego's essence.

Novalis, as will be shown, visualizes the fusion of truth and beauty to be accomplished in the act of artistic representation. Novalis thinks of art as the manifestation of man's essential nature, which brings him into close proximity to Schiller's ideas on aesthetics and the aesthetic education of man. Accordingly, the next section of the present chapter will continue the discussion on truth and beauty by examining the relation between philosophy and art. Thereafter, Novalis' concept of artistic representation will be analyzed, followed by a brief summary of similar aspects in Schiller's views.

C. ARTISTIC REPRESENTATION

The words which most appropriately introduce artistic productivity in terms already familiar are these:

Die Kraft das *Allgemeine* zu denken, ist die philosophische Kraft. Die Kraft, das Besondre zu denken die dichterische. Das Allgemeine ist das Schlechthin schon gesezte - das Besondre, das Beziehungsweise gesezte - oder Jenes die Sfäre, in der etwas gesezt wird - dieses die Sfäre, die *in* jener gesezt wird. Jenes ein Geseztseyn - dieses ein Setzen. /

Seyn drückt das Verhältniss des Ganzen zum Theil, und des Theils zum Ganzen aus./ Totalität und Partialitæt stehen sich entgegen (193, 11-194, 6).

Within the framework of Novalis' schema of interrelation, the characteristics of subjectivity and objectivity become instrumental in identifying the basic aspects of philosophy and art. Novalis points out once again that the empirical ego spans the entire realm of 'being' (*Seyn*); it does so in its dual role as the subjective totality which encompasses all of being, and as the objective part which is the prime unit for the infinite multiplicity of being ("Seyn drückt das Verhältniss des Ganzen zum Theil, und des Theils zum Ganzen aus./Totalität and Partialitæt stehen sich entgegen", 294, 4-6). The realm of the general owes its unity to the ego's ability to harbor its totality, which is just another way of stating what Fichte means when he says: "Es ist demnach Erklärungsgrund aller Thatsachen des empirischen Bewusstseyns, dass vor allem Setzen im Ich vorher das Ich selbst gesetzt sey. - "(*SW*, I, 25). The power manifest in uniting the general is derived from the same absolute unity to which philosophy attempts to lend expression. The empirical ego is the posited sphere from which the general receives its unity ("Das Allgemeine ist das Schlechthin schon gesezte - . . . die Sfäre, in der etwas gesezt wird -" 193, 12-194, 1); philosophy is the reenactment of this positing action in order to trace it to its absolute source ("Die Kraft das *Allgemeine* zu denken ist die philosophische Kraft", 193, 11). Philosophy is explained further under the heading "Unbestimmte Sätze" (113) as an analytical process which takes its course from a given non-objective point of unity transmitted by way of 'feeling': "D[ie] Filosofie soll nicht mehr antworten, als sie gefragt wird. Hervorbringen kann sie nichts. Es muss ihr etwas gegeben werden / Analyse/. Dieses ordnet und erklärt sie" (113, 1-3). "/Die Filosofie ist ursprünglich ein Gefühl. Die Anschauungen dieses Gefühls begreifen die filosofischen Wissenschaften/" (113, 27-28). The axiomatic 'given' thus declared fundamental to philosophic thought is none other than the ego's absolute synthetic function which means the complete identity of thought and being, or in other words, the combined efforts of the theoretical and the practical ego as Fichte envisions it in his *Tathandlung,* referred to as *Urhandlung* by Novalis ("Das dem Gefühl Gegebne scheint mir die Urhandlung als Ursache und Wirkung zu seyn", 114, 3-4). The felt 'given' stands opposed as cause and effect when subject to analysis; unity analyzed is duality, and this dualism relates on a general basis by reason of the absolute unity which is its prime foundation.

The 'power to philosophize' (*philosophische Kraft*) rests, for Novalis, with the ability to reenact consciously (*denken*) the spontaneous, and therefore unreflected, analysis which constitutes the inner world of the ego's subjective moment. The manner of reenactment is the process of externalization ("Die Anschauungen dieses Gefühls begreifen die filosofischen Wissenschaften/" 113, 27-28) which we have already come to know as sign or 'thought perception in terms of sense perception' (*angeschaute Vorstellung*). The ability to communicate significantly carries with it the possibility of communicating significance, or truth per se; that is to say, it carries with it the possibility of philosophical communication. Truth has been defined as a manifestation of the law of association freely produced by the power of the imagination. The communication of truth per se is, therefore, equivalent to communicating the ego's free and absolute nature, which means that the ego's freedom has to be demonstrated empirically. On the level of common experience the ego feels its positing action ("Die Kraft das *Allgemeine* zu denken, ist die philosophische Kraft. Die Kraft, das Besondre zu denken die dichterische . . . Jenes ein Geseztseyn - dieses ein Setzen", 193, 11-194, 3) to be determined by a force other than its own; the causality of any act of perception seems to inhere in the object. It has been pointed out repeatedly that this misapprehension is natural to the empirical ego which is unable to recognize its own freedom. An empirical reenactment of the absolute ego's freedom of action would take place if a sense of productivity were to accompany the ego's relation to objectivity. In Novalis' opinion artistic productivity accomplishes just that, as he states with these words:

Wir erwecken die Thätigkeit, wenn wir ihr reitzenden Stoff geben. / Das Ich muss sich, als darstellend setzen./ Das Wesentliche der Darstellung ist - was das Beywesentliche des Gegenstands ist/ Gibt es eine besondre darstellende Kraft - die blos um darzustellen, darstellt - darstellen, um darzustellen ist ein *Freyes* Darstellen. Es wird damit nur angedeutet, dass nicht das Obj(ect) qua solches sondern *das Ich*, als

Grund der Thätigkeit, die Thätigkeit bestimmen soll. Dadurch erhält das Kunstwerck einen freyen selbstständigen, idealischen Karacter - einen imposanten Geist - denn es ist *sichtbares* Produkt eines Ich - Das Ich aber sezt sich auf diese Art bestimmt, weil es sich, als ein unend-liches Ich sezt - weil es sich, als ein unendlich darstellendes Ich setzen muss - so sezt es sich frey, als ein bestimmt darstellendes Ich. /Das Obj(ect) darf nur der Keim, der Typus seyn, der Vestpunct - die bil-dende Kraft entwickelt an, in und durch ihn erst schöpferisch das schöne Gantze. Anders ausgedrückt - das Object soll uns, als Produkt des Ich, bestimmen, nicht, als blosses Obj[ect]./ (282, 18-34)

The keynote of this passage is that the determinative power of the object is to be abridged, in which respect Novalis is in perfect agreement with Kant and Fichte. He envisions this deobjectification along a pattern similar to the one displayed in art; here he differs from Kant and Fichte, but moves on the other hand in close proxi-mity to Schiller's aesthetic views, as we shall see later. For the moment, we shall restrict ourselves to a detailed exposition of the ideas Novalis conveys in the passage above. Thereafter, a brief discussion on Schiller's concept of the 'play impulse'[19] (*Spieltrieb*) will follow in order to demonstrate how closely related the two positions really are.

Artistic productivity regards its object only as the potential bearer of artistic form which strips the objective realm for the artist of its independent reality. Objectivity becomes transformed into a mold for self-representation which functions simultaneously as sti-mulus and as recipient for the ego's activity ("Wir erwecken die Thätigkeit, wenn wir ihr reitzenden Stoff geben./ Das Ich muss sich, als darstellend setzen./" 282, 18-19). Self-representation means non-determination by any alien influence whatever; if it did not, the objective realm would cease to be representative and as-sume an existence in its own right ("Das Wesentliche der Darstel-lung ist - was das Beywesentliche des Gegenstands ist/" 282, 19-20). Self-identity, which entails the attributes unlimitable, and therefore infinite, absolute, and free, is thus a necessary corollary to self-representation so that the possibility of the artistically re-

[19]   The English term is taken from Reginald Snell's translation: Friedrich Schiller, *On the Aesthetic Education of Man: In a Series of Letters,* Reginald Snell, translator (London, 1954).

presentative act becomes contingent on the reality of an absolute or free ego.

An act is truly self-representative only when all motivation other than the one contained within the representative act itself has been excluded as alien and as directly opposed to representation. The absolute ego can thus further be defined as pure action which is a univocal term for pure self-representation, or representation for the sake of representation ("Gibt es eine besondre darstellende Kraft - die blos um darzustellen, darstellt - darstellen, um darzustellen ist *Freyes* Darstellen", 282, 21-22).

When one particular entity becomes the representative of another, as does the work of art relative to its creator, the result is the active negation of an object's self-identity. The determinative force necessary for such an encroachment is itself unassailed by any of the object's possible actions, and must insofar be pure ("Es wird damit nur angedeutet, dass nicht das Obj(ect) qua solches sondern das Ich, als Grund der Thätigkeit, die Thätigkeit bestimmen soll" 282, 23-25).

Pure action is absolute, which means that there is no other action; yet any particular act of representation, of artistic productivity as it is reflected in the objective realm, differs as an act limited by its object from that very same object as well as from pure action itself. Representation really means self-manifestation in an 'other', since the representative object paradoxically is and is not that which it represents ("Dadurch erhält das Kunstwerk einen freyen, selbstständigen, idealischen Karacter — einen imposanten Geist — denn es ist *sichtbares* Produkt eines Ich -" 228, 25-27). If action consists, artistically speaking, of representation in this sense, then its pure form would be the creation of that very paradox, that is to say, the creation of an 'other' which is representative of its creator. Because pure action is absolute and there is no other realm but its own, creating an 'other' can take place only in the form of limitation, limitation of the self by the self ("Das Ich aber sezt sich auf diese Art bestimmt, weil es sich, als ein unendliches Ich sezt — weil es sich, als ein unendlich darstellendes Ich setzen muss — so sezt es sich frey, als ein bestimmt darstellendes Ich./" 282, 27-30).

If the limited is to represent the unlimited, its action will consist of negating its limit, so that the limiting realm in its turn will have to give up its identity and become representative of the limited realm. The limiter, or object, has existence only insofar as it is to be negated. It can never be entirely negated, because then the original state of absolute action itself would be reached, which is contradictory if absolute action is to be representative action, and if its product is to be not identical with it but representative of it ("Das Obj[ect] darf nur der Keim, der Typus seyn, der Vestpunct - die bildende Kraft entwickelt an, in und durch ihn erst schöpferisch das schöne Gantze", 282, 30-32).

In this way, the object of artistic endeavors exists for artistic creativity only as its potential product, and that it can be only if it is a product of that creativity to begin with. This does not mean that the artist creates the material he works with *ex nihilo;* it merely indicates that the artist has to apply receptivity of artistic form as criterion to the objective realm by means of which he detaches the particulars of his choice from their objective continuum ("Anders ausgedrückt - das Object soll uns, als Produkt des Ich, bestimmen, nicht, als blosses Obj[ect]./" 282, 32-34).

It has now become obvious that it is not possible to restrict these arguments entirely to art. The formative aspect so pronounced in artistic productivity is really basic to the most elemental relationship, that of subject to object, in the manner Fichte conceives it to be. In this connection, the following words will demonstrate further that Novalis quite consciously tends to interpret Fichte's philosophy as a universal aesthetics:

<Es wäre wohl möglich, dass Fichte Erfinder einer ganz neuen Art zu denken wäre - für die die Sprache noch keinen Namen hat. Der Erfinder ist vielleicht nicht der fertigste und sinnreichste Künstler auf seinem Instrument - ob ich gleich nicht sage, dass es so sey - Es ist aber wahrscheinlich, dass es Menschen giebt und geben wird - die weit besser Fichtisiren werden, als Fichte. Es können *wunderbare Kunstwercke* hier entstehen - wenn man das Fichtisiren erst artistisch zu treiben beginnt.> (524, 8-15)

These words were taken from a collection of philosophic fragments entitled "Logologische Fragmente". They were written in the early part of 1798,[20] not quite three years after *Letters Concerning the*

[20] Kl², II, 751.

Aesthetic Education of Man (Über die ästhetische Erziehung des Menschen, in einer Reihe von Briefen) had appeared in Schiller's periodical *Die Horen*.[21] Their author, Schiller himself, is, like Novalis, conscious of Fichte's potential importance to the theory of aesthetics. Consequently, the *Wissenschaftslehre* is mentioned directly[22] and implicitly[23] in *The Letters,* despite the fact that they are otherwise constructed entirely around Kantian philosophy and terminology.[24] Their basic goal is a modulation of Kant's apparent moralistic rigor[25] by means of the mediating function the aesthetic exercises with respect to the rational (*Vernunft*) and the sensual (*Sinnlichkeit*), to duty (*Pflicht*) and inclination (*Neigung*): "Der Nothwendigkeit strenge Stimme, die Pflicht, muss ihre vorwerfende Formel verändern, die nur der Widerstand rechtfertigt, und die wil-

---

[21] *Die Horen,* Nos. 1, 2, and 6; Fr. Schiller, editor (Jena, 1795). Any references made to Schiller's writings will henceforth refer to: *Schillers Werke,* Nationalausgabe (Weimar, 1943-), and will be abbreviated as Schiller, Vol., p.

[22] "(Diesen Begriff der Wechselwirkung und die ganze Wichtigkeit desselben findet man vortrefflich auseinandergesetzt in Fichte's Grundlage der gesammten Wissenschaftslehre, Leipzig 1794)", Vol. XX, p. 348.

[23] That is, the use of the term *Tathandlung* in the following passage: "Aber aus einer blossen Ausschliessung würde in Ewigkeit keine Realität und aus einer blossen Sinnenempfindung in Ewigkeit keine Vorstellung werden, wenn nicht Etwas vorhanden wäre, von welchem ausgeschlossen wird, wenn nicht durch eine absolute Thathandlung des Geistes die Negation auf etwas Positives bezogen, und aus Nichtsetzung Entgegensetzung würde; diese Handlung des Gemüths heisst urtheilen oder denken, und das Resultat derselben der Gedanke" (Vol. XX, p. 369).

[24] The central importance of the terms 'stuff' (*Stoff*) and 'form' (*Form*) points to Reinhold of whom Nikolai Hartmann says: "Der Gedanke der Vernunftkritik geht für ihn nahezu auf in zwei Begriffspaaren: Form und Stoff einerseits, Erscheinung und Ding an sich andererseits" (*Die Philosophie des Deutschen Idealismus* [Berlin, 1960], p. 8). Schiller seems to have carried this process of simplification one step further by reducing his basic framework to the former pair of opposites exclusively.

[25] Schiller, Vol. XX, p. 348: "In einer Transcendental-Philosophie, wo alles darauf ankommt, die Form von dem Inhalt zu befreyen und das Nothwendige von allem Zufälligen rein zu erhalten, gewöhnt man sich gar leicht, das Materielle sich bloss als Hindernis zu denken und die Sinnlichkeit, weil sie gerade bey diesem Geschäft im Wege steht, in einem nothwendigen Widerspruch mit der Vernunft vorzustellen. Eine solche Vorstellungsart liegt zwar auf keine Weise im Geiste des Kantischen Systems, aber im Buchstaben desselben könnte sie gar wohl liegen."

lige Natur durch ein edleres Zutrauen ehren."[26] Let us now briefly examine the ideological environment to which this last statement refers, after which the *Letters* themselves and their relevance to Novalis' view will be discussed in more detail.

It is wellknown that Kant's critical bulwark, with which he tried to protect "those majestic ethical edifices" against the inroads of skepticism, resulted in a redistribution of authority between subject and object, and left the latter much the poorer for it. The subject's endowment with practical reason (*praktische Vernunft*) made it possible to declare its sovereignty as an ethical being, and this intimate connection between ethics and freedom set the tone for the philosophical climate of German Idealism.[27] From the moralist's point of view, freedom will manifest itself in that human behavior which involves no manner of determination from the objective realm. This essentially negative criterion is espoused by Kant when he denies ethical validity to an act committed according to inclination (*Neigung*) rather than duty (*Pflicht*). The subject's freedom has to be tried and proven by means of confrontation with the contrary demands of the object. Even Fichte cannot avoid this clash, since he too has actually no other aim but the justification of ethics. He bestows absolute freedom on the subject by eliminating the

---

[26]   Schiller, Vol. XX, pp. 411-412. The same dissatisfaction on Schiller's part with the demands made in the *Critique of Practical Reason (Kritik der praktischen Vernunft)*, that moral acts cannot be accompanied by inclination, gave rise to these lines: "Gerne dien' ich den Freunden, doch tu ich es leider mit Neigung, Und so wurmt es mich oft, dass ich nicht tugendhaft bin" ("Xenien", No. 388).

[27]   As Nicolai Hartmann points out in his work: "Die Möglichkeit der sittlich freien Handlung und das Postulat einer moralischen Weltordnung erwiesen sich als philosophisch haltbar durch die an der theoretischen Vernunft geübten Kritik. Davon war Reinhold in seinen Briefen über die Kantische Philosophie ausgegangen. Aber er hatte es nicht verstanden, diesen bei Kant gross angelegten Gedanken über das populäre Interesse der religiösen Aufklärung energisch herauszuheben und ihn zum Zentralpunkt des philosophischen Weltbildes zu machen" (p. 41). "Fichte ist in seinem philosophischen Grundinteresse Reinhold eng verwandt. Auch er kommt durchaus von der ethisch-religiösen Seite auf die Kantische Philosophie. Aber er geht von vornherein viel zentraler auf ihr Ganzes, auf ihren inneren, ungeschriebenen Kernpunkt. Nicht mehr das Werk des Kritizismus als solches ist ihm wesentlich, sondern durchaus nur der Gedanke der tathaften moralischen Ursprünglichkeit des Menschenwesens, an dem alle metaphysischen Schranken und Fesseln eines deterministisch gebundenen Naturwesens im Menschen aufspringen und den Ausblick ins Absolute auftun" (p. 42).

thing in itself, the last remnant of objectivity, only in order to
restore the world of objects in its entirety as the ethical proving
ground for the ego's practical assets.[28]

Critical Philosophy decides the relation between subject and
object in favor of the former, and in doing so merely reaffirms the
sense of difference and disharmony between the two for the individual who is confronted with the task of realizing this 'decision'
empirically. Ethics has been saved as Kant intended, but with it the
clash between spirit and flesh, or rather between duty and inclination, as the new formulation would have it, has also been preserved.
In one area, however, a true harmony was discovered, and that was
in the realm of aesthetics. The state of balance between duty and
inclination which Goethe[29] as well as Schiller[30] considered ideal
found expression in the concept of 'the beautiful soul' (*schöne
Seele*). In the same spirit the term *kalokagathia* stands for the fusion
of goodness and harmonious beauty as the maxim underlying German Classicism. The major part of Schiller's philosophic speculations circle around the polarity nature-spirit in numerous attempts
to view its fundamental unison from different perspectives. The
keynote of these efforts, beginning with his 'Elevenarbeit', is to
define the sphere of each with respect to the other, and to establish
between them the aesthetic harmony of reciprocal interdependence.
The balance he envisions is probably best expressed in these words
from his *Letters*: "... es gibt keinen anderen Weg, den sinnlichen
Menschen vernünftig zu machen, als dass man denselben zuvor äs-
thetisch macht".[31] This path clearly marks the aesthetic as point of
unity between the polar stress of sense and reason.[32] The same point

---

[28] Fichte's moralistic tendency is more obvious in his "popular" writings
than in the *Wissenschaftslehre* itself. It is already quite clearly pronounced
in his tract on the *Bestimmung des Menschen*, where, in the third part, he
reestablishes by means of 'faith' (*Glaube*) the reality of the objective realm
solely as a device necessary for ethical practice.
[29] Goethe exposes his ideas on this subject most particularly in that part
of *Wilhelm Meisters Lehrjahre* which bears the title "Bekenntnisse einer
schönen Seele".
[30] Schiller's theory is best expressed in the *Letters Concerning the Aesthetic
Education of Man*, and in his essay, *On Grace and Dignity (Über Anmuth
und Würde)*, Vol. XX, pp. 251-412.
[31] Schiller, Vol. XX, p. 383.
[32] *Vernunft* in the Kantian sense.

of unity is held by the empirical ego with respect to its theoretical and practical functions, which merely signify the ego's dual directedness toward the thing in itself and toward the ultimate criterion of practical reason.[33] The truly human is, therefore, harmony or the aesthetic; Schiller does, in this sense, proclaim the free point of departure in either direction as the aesthetic stage, and art as the manifestation of the perfect harmony which ideally[34] is man.

In this light, a work of art, something not dedicated to any purpose, something merely representative of the unity of the empirical ego, accomplishes the perfect balance of spirit and matter. This is how Schiller expresses it when he discusses the 'aesthetic drive':

Der sinnliche Trieb will bestimmt werden, er will sein Objekt empfangen; der Formtrieb will selbst bestimmen, er will sein Objekt hervorbringen: der Spieltrieb wird also bestrebt sein, so zu empfangen, wie er selbst hervorgebracht hätte, und so hervorzubringen, wie der Sinn zu empfangen trachtet (Vol. XX, p. 354).

The reason for the choice of name (Spieltrieb) is clear: no purpose other than that of representation is permitted to mar the reflection of the essentially human. Purposefulness is a characteristic of man's relation to the material world, and although every rational (vernünftig) or moral action reflects 'personality' (Persönlichkeit),[35]

---

[33]   Both constitute merely directions, i.e., negative values, because neither enters as such the realm of appearances; they determine it, nonetheless, insofar as it is their common ground.

[34]   In actuality, the aesthetic stage would constitute 'the beautiful soul', man as a perfect work of art. Works of art hold up the image of that harmony which man must attain to become himself.

[35]   Persönlichkeit in the sense in which Schiller employs it refers to the essentially human quality within man as opposed to those qualities he shares with all other being. The most apt example of 'personality' in Kantian terms would be an individual's ability to act according to the dictates of the Categorical Imperative, rather than his being compelled exclusively by the motivations arising from physical existence. This is Schiller's interpretation: "Der zweyte jener Triebe, den man den Formtrieb nennen kann, geht aus von dem absoluten Daseyn des Menschen oder von seiner vernünftigen Natur und ist bestrebt, ihn in Freyheit zu setzen, Harmonie in die Verschiedenheit seines Erscheinens zu bringen und bey allem Wechsel des Zustands seine Person zu behaupten. Da nun die letztere als absolute und untheilbare Einheit mit sich selbst nie in Widerspruch seyn kann, da wir in alle Ewigkeit wir sind, so kann der jenige Trieb, der auf Behauptung der Persönlichkeit dringt, nie etwas anders fordern, als was er in alle Ewigkeit fordern muss; er entschei-

it does so only with respect to the particular individual's existence which happens to be material. The material drive has its purposes in the realm of physical existence; the form-drive has its purposes in the formation of matter according to human form, which is essentially equivalent to the elimination of matter in its own right. In this case, however, the matter is man whom the form-drive cannot eliminate without destroying itself, a measure taken in extreme cases only.[36] Singularly the aesthetic drive is not in any way concerned with the existence of man in creation: it merely represents the essentially human. Even in a work of art, allowances have to be made for material conditions. However, these material conditions (not of man's making) have no essential bearing on the representative function of the object, except insofar as they are re-formed. Matter in this case expresses form only and in being thus 'entirely' removed from the material world lies the purposelessness of the artistic creation. Schiller expresses the relation of form to matter in these words:

Darin also besteht das eigentliche Kunstgeheimniss des Meisters, *dass er den Stoff durch die Form vertilgt;* and je imposanter, anmassender, verführerischer der Stoff an sich selbst ist, je eigenmächtiger derselbe mit *seiner* Wirkung sich vordrängt, oder je mehr der Betrachter geneigt ist, sich unmittelbar mit dem Stoff einzulassen, desto triumphirender ist die Kunst, welche jenen zurückzwingt und über diesen die Herrschaft behauptet (Vol. XX, p. 382).

The two basic drives when applied with respect to the 'person's' existence in the material world will always be mutually exclusive.[37] The form of the 'formless' flux of matter is not of the human spirit and therefore, man in the state of sensation is devoid of 'personality', whereas the operation of the mind excludes all 'formlessness' or other form. As long as man is bound to matter for his existence, this dualism will prevail. Only when man is in no way preoccupied with his existence, when he acts entirely without purposes, may he

---

det also für immer, wie er für jetzt entscheidet, und gebietet für jetzt, was er für immer gebietet" (Vol. XX, pp. 345-346). Also Novalis' concept of 'person' is entirely in accordance with Schiller's definition: "Vollendeter Mensch — Person, zu seyn — das ist die Bestimmung und der Urtrieb im Menschen" (165, 27-28).
[36]   The tragic hero, for instance.
[37]   With the exception of 'the beautiful soul', of course.

form a segment of the flux in time and space so that in addition
to its fragmentary significance in the infinite realm of nature, which
is entirely eliminated because of the purposelessness of the action,
it will bear the law of the human mind and reflect its form. Because
of the lack of purpose, any material aspects as material aspects
lose their meaning (or rather meaninglessness in the sense of 'formlessness'), and any sensual contact kept free of purpose[38] will experience the phenomenalized form of man. Purely physical action
is man in terms of nature; rational (*vernünftig*) action is nature in
terms of man. Aesthetic action, however, is man in terms of man.

Now it may become more apparent why Fichtean philosophy
plays such a noticeable part in the *Letters,* a fact which Kuno
Fischer mentions in these words:

Aber nicht blos von einzelnen Stellen, sondern von der ganzen Deduc-
tion der ästhetischen Freiheit aus dem Ich und seinen Grundtrieben,
wie überhaupt von der zweiten Gruppe der Briefe insgesammt (X-XVI)
darf dieser Einfluss gelten. Nie hat Schiller der Wissenschaftslehre
näher gestanden, als in dem Zeitpunkt, wo er diese Briefe schrieb. Es
war im Herbst 1794.[39]

Schiller's aesthetic theories bring about a shift in the crucial relationship between subject and object which coincides with the one
effected by Fichte's philosophy. Both eliminate the object's independence, the 'thing in itself'. The poet designates that point at
which man gains his freedom the aesthetic stage where objectivity
becomes merely a name for the potential mirror of man; the philosopher makes that same freedom the very fountainhead of empirical existence, and all of objectivity is posited only as the potential
reflector of man's freedom. Both men were essentially moralists.
Fichte considered himself Kant's apostle bent on the very same
mission which gave rise to Critical Philosophy in the first place, and
Schiller never ceased to think of the stage as anything but a 'moral
institution'. To him, art is still subservient to ethics, not in the crude
and direct fashion of the Enlightenment where it serves as the
aesthetically delectable shell for a moralistic core, but rather as
the projected image of that harmony of soul which is the prerequi-

---

[38]   Avoidance of making the object a target for physical desire.
[39]   Kuno Fischer, *Schiller als Philosoph* (2d ed.; Heidelberg, 1891), p. 296.

site for ethical conduct. Fichte absolutizes that same fusion of the practical and theoretical, which comprises Schiller's *Spieltrieb*, in his concept of *Tathandlung* as the axiom from which all else follows. Although Fichte's motives are like those of Kant in the interest of ethics, he inadvertently also offers in his philosophy the possibility of absolutizing the *Spieltrieb, i.e.,* aesthetics, as well. The absolute action referred to in the *Tathandlung* only has to be thought of as representative action, and Novalis has done just that in his "Fichte Studies".

IV

CONCLUSION

A. SUMMARY STATEMENT

Before we turn to the question of whether the ideas contained in the "Fichte Studies" can be considered to have had any effect on Novalis' later development as artist and thinker, it would seem advantageous to summarize briefly the findings and implications of the previous chapters.

The basic dualism of empirical reality, the fundamental dichotomy of subject and object, was found to entail a relationship, or unity, despite the forbidding gulf which allows for either member in a sphere of mutually exclusive isolation only. No all-inclusive third sphere could be located as basis for this unity nor even a point of mutual limitation or tangency; the all-inclusive sphere and the point of mutual limitation could be postulated only as the Absolute and the empirical ego, respectively. All that was found was a definite correspondence between the subjective and objective realms so that either became the image of the other. The factuality of this reciprocal correspondence was shown to be contingent on a point of mutual limitation and origin. The term 'empirical ego', it was noted, describes this very point in its twofold capacity as both boundary and gateway to the dual expanse of subject and object, whereas the terms 'absolute ego' or 'God' were used by Novalis to convey the 'idea' of that total sphere which the infinity of subject and object attempts to fill in vain. Without the idea of a total sphere as a potential reference point, the empirical ego could not function as the center for the infinite bilateral extension of subject and object. Thus God is manifest in the empirical ego which is in turn manifest in the reciprocal relation which exists between subjectivity and objectivity, between the reality of self and nature. Since subject and object are related in this manner, neither can maintain the state of isolated self-identity suggested by its 'otherness'. On the contrary, the finite unity attributable to each, by reason of the exclusive confinement which separation entails, is broken continually in order to allow the subject to be inclusive of the object and vice versa, so that each is manifest in the other. 'Subject' and 'object' are concepts as elusive as 'God' and 'empirical ego', so that no defined certainty is left but the certainty of their mutual interdependence within which no one instance ever remains immutably fixed. This idea finds very fitting expression in the metaphor of the following quotation. Novalis uses the term 'thing' (*Ding*) in order to refer to both the extensive and intensive, *i.e.*, the objective and subjective realms; the term 'common realm of origin' *(gemeinschaftlicher Bezirk des Grundes)* refers to that which we have called 'empirical ego', and the term 'whole' (*das Ganze*) is synonymous with Absolute:

Alles Ding, ist, wie aller Grund, relativ. Er ist Ding, insofern sein Entgegengeseztes Ding ist - Sie sind beyde nicht Dinge, insofern sie im gemeinschaftlichen Bezirk des Grundes sind - der dann Ding ist. Jedes Ding steckt im höheren Dinge, oder weitern - extensivern und intensivern Dinge -/extens[iv] und intens[iv] müssen eigentlich Einer Handlung Produkt seyn, wie Position und Negation/ Nur das Ganze ist *real* - Nur das Ding wäre absolut real, das nicht wieder *Bestandtheil* wäre. Das Ganze ruht ohngefähr - wie die spielenden Personen, die sich ohne Stuhl, blos Eine auf der andern Knie kreisförmig hinsetzen (p. 242, 18-28).

The schema of interrelation, where the ego is the image of nature, nature the image of the ego, and the relation between the two the image of the nameless Absolute, is obviously not a static condition, but constitutes rather a dynamic relationship which we came to know as representative action (*Darstellung*). In the course of our discussion on the topic of representation (*Darstellung*), it was found that the absolute ego is free action or absolute form, and thus self-limited absolute content. As absolute content it is, again, nothing but its own self, that is, form and content. The difference is that the relativized absolute power of the ego, its form-giving aspect within the absolute contentual realm, is now limited. Limitation at this stage is experienced as the expandability of the relative content beyond the boundary of form. Novalis refers to it as the 'external-ization of content' ("Weil das Ich ein durchgehends bestimmtes ist, so kann es den allgemeinen Gehalt nur in sich erkennen. Inwiefern es den allgemeinen Gehalt ausser sich versezt - muss es daran glauben", 105, 8-10). Whereas in the absolute realm per se content was dependent on free unlimited activity, the situation has become reversed in the absolute contentual realm: here form-giving activity, the uniform sphere of consciousness or knowledge, is 'felt' ("Was ich nicht weis, aber fühle/das Ich fühlt sich selbst, als Gehalt / glaube ich", 105, 11-13) to be dependent on the infinite externa-lized content. Since this external realm is called 'being', the ego 'is' insofar as it depends on it in its formative or knowing function.[1] Form and content are really only different terms for the same con-cepts which had previously been introduced as 'analysis' and 'syn-thesis', respectively.[2] Absolute content entails relative form and content; it is the empirical realm with its aspects of subjectivity and objectivity in its analytic and synthetic approach towards infinity.

Novalis' emphasis on 'being' (Seyn) establishes a balance be-tween self and world where Fichte's speculations, which concen-trate on the Ego's active or formative aspect exclusively, appeared to have left nothing but a disproportion bordering on solipsism. However, this balance is brought about entirely by means of the Fichtean concepts of 'feeling' (Gefühl) and faith (Glaube) which, as we noted, are used by that philosopher to escape complete iso-lation within the ego. It is Fichte's moralistic tendency which leads to his one-sided preoccupation with the ego as source of action, to the point of bypassing the 'world' merely as the potential elicitor of moral action. In his tract "Die Bestimmung des Menschen", which was to be a popular exposition of the major tenets contained in the Wissenschaftslehre, Fichte claims in effect that reality, order, and, above all, existence of the world are only with respect to the sub-ject's possible action, that is, its ethos. A person's conscious pro-duction of the world (Vorstellung) is according to the ethical duty

---

[1] "Was für eine Beziehung ist das Wissen? Es ist ein Seyn ausser dem Seyn, das doch im Seyn ist. /Theilen-vereinen/Das Bewusstsein ist ein Seyn ausser dem Seyn im Seyn ... D[as] Bewusstseyn ist folglich ein Bild des Seyns im Seyn" (106, 1-9).

[2] C.f. chap. ii.

he has to enact in it.[3] Novalis, to be sure, stays within the Fichtean framework, only his accentuation is more evenly distributed between self and world, since he never loses sight of the Absolute's 'form-contentual' aspect, or, in Fichte's terms, he never forgets that *Tathandlung* comprises *Tat* as well as *handeln,* content as well as form. For him, the absolute unity of form and content is reflected in the unity of the reciprocal relation between empirical form and content where 'being' (*Seyn*) relates to knowledge as absolute content does to absolute form, with the critical difference, however, that in the latter relation form determines content, whereas in the former one content is 'felt' to be independent of form. Fichte's Absolute is the Ego, source of spontaneity which results empirically in the possibility of ethical action; but Novalis can call the Absolute both God and Ego in one and the same breath, since his state of the empirical is the simultaneity of action and passion, spirit and 'being', form and content, where both paths reach out to the same Infinity and where a change in name is merely indicative of the direction from which the Absolute is approached.

Fichte's moralistic fervor leads him in his philosophy to divest objectivity of any independent integrity. The implications of this position with respect to aesthetics were not lost on Novalis, as has been shown. Mention was made of the basic relation between ethics and aesthetics implicit in Kant's Critical Philosophy which Schiller formulated explicitly in his concept of 'play instinct' (*Spieltrieb*); Fichte's absolute act (*Tathandlung*), the guarantor of ethics, proved to be the very same vision of freedom made possible only by the moment of indifference between subject and object.[4] With Novalis,

[3] "... kein Wissen kann sich selbst begründen und beweisen; jedes Wissen setzt ein noch Höheres voraus, als seinen Grund, und dieses Aufsteigen hat kein Ende. Der *Glaube* ist es; dieses freiwillige Beruhen bei der sich uns natürlich darbietenden Ansicht, weil wir nur bei dieser Ansicht unsere Bestimmung erfüllen können; er ist es, der dem Wissen erst Beifall gibt, und das, was ohne ihn blosse Täuschung sein könnte, zur Gewissheit und Überzeugung erhebt. *Er ist kein Wissen, sondern ein Entschluss des Willens, das Wissen gelten zu lassen*" (*SW*, II, 253).
[4] The second edition of the *Wissenschaftslehre* bears this footnote after the concept of *Tathandlung* has been developed in the first basic axiom ('erster schlechthin unbedingter Grundsatz'): "Dies Alles heisst nun mit anderen Worten, mit denen ich es seitdem ausgedrückt habe: *Ich* ist notwendig Identität des Subjects und Objects; Subject-Object: und dies ist es schlechthin ohne weitere Vermittlung. Dies, sage ich, heisst es; ohnerachtet dieser

both Fichte's absolute version of this moment and Schiller's relative one become united and are transformed into the absolute aesthetics which we have found in the "Fichte Studies".

B. CONCLUDING REMARKS

Insofar as the philosophic fragments of the "Fichte Studies" are from an early phase of the author's development, they cannot constitute any final authority, but there are definite indications that the basic position, as formulated in the present discussion, continues to be of determinative value.

Many efforts have been made to formulate either qualitatively or quantitatively the sum total of Friedrich von Hardenberg's intellectual and spiritual concerns. While it is impossible to point to any one opinion as irrefutable and definitive, a representative selection of highly reputable analyses made from entirely different perspectives of professional interest does show striking agreement in one particular area. Whether his work be examined in order to determine its theological significance or its pertinence to the science of mathematics or its evaluation of history or its place in the literary tradition of the Occident, his concept of unity will always determine any conclusions that may have been reached. It is a matter of commonplace knowledge reduced to a cliché that Novalis envisions world and self as one; how he envisions this miraculous fusion is a question which cannot be answered with glib facility. It is actually the question which lies at the core of all inquiry into his writings, and the theological inquiry made by Karl Barth,[5] the mathematical inquiry made by Käte Hamburger,[6] the historical inquiry made by Wilfried Malsch,[7] and the literary inquiry made by Hans-Joachim Mähl[8] form no exception.

Satz nicht so leicht eingesehen und nach seiner hohen, vor der W. L. durchgängig vernachlässigten Wichtigkeit erwogen ist, als man denken möchte; daher die vorhergehenden Erörterungen desselben nicht erlassen werden können" (*SW*, I, 98).

[5] *Die protestantische Theologie.*
[6] "Novalis und die Mathematik".
[7] *"Europa": Poetische Rede des Novalis* (Stuttgart, 1965).
[8] *Die Idee des goldenen Zeitalters im Werk des Novalis* (Stuttgart, 1965).

Karl Barth approaches his material in a manner similar to the one in which we approached the "Fichte Studies", and he does so for the same reason. Of the dichotomies which occur throughout Novalis' work he selects those most universally applicable in order to use them as guides for general orientation only because, as he puts it, "eine Darstellung der Gedankenwelt des Novalis ist m. E. ein Ding der Unmöglichkeit, oder eben ein Ding, des nur ein wiederkehrender Novalis selber vollbringen könnte" (p. 310). His findings have an equally familiar ring; he concludes that Novalis' dichotomies point to a concept of the empirical ego as the neutral ground of mediation between an external and an internal infinity by divine decree (p. 313). The fragmentary annotation, made either in 1798 or in 1799, "Gott ist bald $1.\infty$, bald $\frac{1}{\infty}$, bald O"[9] seems to Karl Barth most succinctly expressive of Novalis' general position; however, it is now obvious that this laconic formula constitutes an apt summation of a conceptual framework which emerges already several years earlier in the "Fichte Studies". For Karl Barth, Novalis' point of view entails the grave danger of confusing the Absolute and the empirical, the divine and the merely human, or as he puts it, of substituting Christ for Mary (p. 339). The problem which the theologian poses for himself loses its authenticity when Novalis' ideas are examined as originating with his reflections on Fichtean philosophy where, as the previous chapters have shown, the relation between the Absolute and the empirical state is envisioned as a mutually representative schema of interrelation which simultaneously allows for the complete integrity of each participant as well as for ultimate unity.

The relevancy of Käte Hamburger's essay to the present discussion has already been pointed out in a previous chapter.[10] In her presentation it becomes clear that Novalis considers the principles of calculus to be a symbolic expression of the empirical ego's own reality, and reference to it as the integral and differential of the universe[11] signifies the same relationship which we have described

[9] Ernst Kamnitzer (ed.), *Novalis Fragmente* (Dresden, 1928). May be found in Kl¹, III, 247.
[10] Pp. 45-46.
[11] Kl¹, III, 103. Käte Hamburger puts a great deal of emphasis on this fragment (p. 150 ff).

as the ego's binary relation to infinity. Here again it becomes quite evident that the pattern of unity as it is shaped in the "Fichte Studies" furnishes the basis for studies and reflections which preoccupy Novalis long after 1796.

Novalis' view of history, as it emerges from Wilfried Malsch's consideration of *Die Christenheit oder Europa,* attributes the temporal continuity of the historical process to the synthesizing unity of the human spirit which is ultimately derived from the Absolute. This spiritual present (*'geistige Gegenwart'*) in contrast to the experienced present sets up the standard of ideal unity according to which all historical action and all government should be patterned in an asymptotic effort at emulation. Again we encounter the empirical ego as the absolutely decreed point of tangency for a dualistic infinity which originates with a decree of equal authority, only this time in terms of the ego's historical expanse into past and future rather than in the terms of inner world and outer world or self and nature.

The concept of an historical continuum is also essential to Hans-Joachim Mähl's exemplary work of literary analysis, *Die Idee des goldenen Zeitalters im Werk des Novalis.* There he traces the *topos* of the 'golden age' from Hesiod to the 18th century in a most successful effort to circumscribe Novalis' own contributions to the theme and thus to clarify his poetic intention. Germinal to this intention is Novalis' insistence on the reciprocity of spheres as the necessary requisite for representation (p. 300). The seemingly opposing spheres of the spirit and of the senses are viewed as representative of one another, a view which presupposes their ultimate unity in an absolute sphere. The absolute sphere is in its turn represented by the related dualism of the inner world of the spirit and the outer world of the senses. The same polar opposition which divides space into an inner and an outer sphere is manifest if empirical reality is viewed from the perspective of time. Just as opposition in space constitutes a reciprocal relationship ultimately founded on unity, the opposing spheres of past and future are joined in a true tangential present, the spiritual present (*'geistige Gegenwart')* already mentioned, which establishes a point for the potential realization of the absolute unity of time. Hans-Joachim Mähl calls the pattern of reciprocal polarity the key to the law which governs Novalis' thought and being (". . . ein Schlüsselgesetz des Novalis, eine ständig wiederkehrende Denk- und Seinsform seines eigentümlichen Wesens . . ." p. 318), and he considers the recurring vision of a 'golden age' in Novalis' writings the most pertinent poetic formulation for the spiritual reality of absolute unity upon which that law of reciprocal polarity rests (p. 328). The term 'spiritual present' is now interpreted to mean the simultaneity of all temporal as well as spatial aspects at a point of tangency which is called 'poetic self-consciousness' *(dichterisches Selbstbewusstsein)* where the unity of the totality of time is said to become inner reality here and now (p. 319). Poetizing, as it is understood by Novalis, is an act which allows for the interpenetration of empirical and supraempirical realities (p. 331). Such an act cannot be contemplated unless it be from a vantage point which places the ego into a central position of mediation as outlined by the schema of interrelation and its dynamics which we found to be the essence of the "Fichte Studies". The theme struck in all of Novalis' works but most elaborately in his last one, *Heinrich von Ofterdingen,* is that of the 'golden age'. It is the symbol of absolute reality wrought by the poet as he describes his own function as seer and mediator from an intellectual position guaranteed him only by the philosophical efforts of the years 1795 and 1796.

It has become sufficiently evident that the "Fichte Studies" by no means represent an isolated set of nebulous speculations having little bearing on their author's later intellectual and artistic activity. They constitute Novalis' most serious attempt to understand and formulate the implications inherent in the fact of his own being, and his resultant insights not only fit into the context of his later pursuits, but actually form their ideological foundation which, as the works by Barth, Hamburger, Malsch, and Mähl exemplify, may be refined or expanded but never altered.

The theoretical struggles reflected in the "Fichte Studies" never crystallize into the fixed formula of a system; they result rather in a spiritual perspective from which the prosaic detail of life appears in the light of its absolute origin. The view thus offered to the beholder fortunate enough to have reached the thin precipice which marks the mutual boundary of self and non-self is one of a world transformed from the dead jumble of an infinite multiplicity born of the empirical realm's basic dualism into the living coherence of an organism where each part reflects the whole. The world remade in this manner is the poetized world which Novalis proclaims in 1798 (Kl[1], II, 335), and which he began to describe as path and fulfilled vision in *Heinrich von Ofterdingen*. The ideas which were generated in the "Fichte Studies" culminate in a novel where the hero's path to his true self concurrently leads to his becoming a true artist. 'Man' and 'artist' are identical terms for Novalis, because both refer to the central point of mediation at which unity and duality merge. It is the only point from which the original act of self-manifestation can be reenacted, an accomplishment performed by the 'man-artist' in the symbolic representation of the only thing representable, the process of representation itself. Only the absolute process of representation as it is reflected in the empirical individual's reenactment of it can furnish material for artistic expression: artistic enactment and artistic result have been merged into one, into an artistic *Tathandlung*.

It is evident that Novalis' thought as well as his practice point in the direction of modern symbolism, and it would therefore seem profitable to consider briefly the possible implications the "Fichte Studies" hold with respect to this movement.

Werner Vordtriede's recent evaluation of Novalis' importance to French Symbolism points out convincingly that advocates of pure art like Baudelaire and Mallarmé relied greatly on that tradition of German Romanticism which had been shaped by the author of *Heinrich von Ofterdingen*. As the subtitle *Zur Entstehungsgeschichte des dichterischen Symbols* indicates, the discussion is essentially concerned with Novalis' use of the symbol and its decisive role in a literary tradition which finds its culmination in French Symbolism. The central topic of Vordtriede's discussion is broached right at the beginning. He establishes the widespread influence of German Romanticism in France as an unprecedented break with French literary tradition, and he considers it a phenomenon linked inextricably with the increasing estrangement of the artist and his product from the actualities of life. The poet's message found an ever growing number of deft ears, so that he was ultimately confronted with the problematic task of justifying himself to himself (p. 13). Central to Vordtriede's discussions are, therefore, both the artist's withdrawal from external reality into the poet's 'inorganic and eternal magic realm'[12] as well as its complementary aspect, his growing preoccupation with himself and his ambivalent relation to life.[13] That this state of complete estrangement is, in fact, the outcome of Europe's intellectual development, and that its roots lie buried in that era of contrast and ferment which Korff collectivized under the name of its greatest representative,[14] must be considered a valid interpretation of cultural history. In his collection of essays, so appropriately entitled *The Disinherited Mind*,[15] Erich Heller has illuminated from a variety of perspectives that very process of disintegration as the ever widening gap between value and reality, and his interpretation has found general acceptance amongst scholars.

If it is not Vordtriede's novel achievement to have outlined the dynamics and the progress of art's isolation in modern times, he is definitely to be credited with the extremely valuable contribution of having determined Novalis' place with respect to it: he has the artist begin his 'journey into the interior'[16] with Novalis' descent into the nether realm of "Klingsohr's Tale".[17]

What initiates this estrangement, this loss of audience, this general exodus from external reality, is the question which inadvertent-

[12] "Wir sind in den künstlichen Garten, das anorganische, unverwesliche Zauberreich des Dichters eingetreten. Wir kennen diesen Garten aus Klingsohrs Märchen, wo, tief unter der Erde, metallne Blumen wachsen, gesondert von der erstarrten und erlösungsbedürftigen Vernunftwelt des Arcturus. Zwar ist das künstliche Dichterreich bei Novalis noch kein Verbannungsort, kein Platz der Verdammten, Frevelhaften und Unfruchtbaren" (p. 21).

[13] Vordtriede quotes from Jean Paul's *Vorschule der Aesthetik*: "Daher suchen dichtende Jünglinge, diese Nachbarn der Nihilisten, z.B. eben Novalis oder auch Kunst-Romanschreiber, sich gern einen Dichter oder Maler oder anderen Künstler zum darstellenden Helden aus, weil sie in dessen weiten, alle Darstellung umfassenden Künstlerraum alles, ihr eigenes Herz, jede Ansicht und Empfindung kunstgerecht niederlegen können; sie liefern daher lieber einen Dichter als ein Gedicht." He continues on his own: "Es ist, als hätte Jean Paul geahnt, dass von nun an in immerzunehmendem Mass der Dichter sich selber reflektieren wird und seine eigene Existenz zum fast ausschliesslichen Inhalt seines Werkes machen wird" (p. 22).

[14] *Geist der Goethezeit.*

[15] Cleveland, 1959. Actually, this work sets the beginning phase of our modern dilemma in the Renaissance; for the present the most determinative instance of the post-medieval trend is, however, the Goethe Era. The essay most applicable to this discussion is "The Hazard of Modern Poetry".

[16] Erich Heller, *The Artist's Journey into the Interior* (New York, 1965).

[17] Vordtriede, p. 21.

ly presents itself to the reader of *Novalis und die französischen
Symbolisten*. Vordtriede documents the process as a factual development in France, beginning with Vigny,[18] and as a post-medieval
problem for Germany[19] which reaches a crisis in the late 18th century, where Goethe's *Tasso* marks the beginning of that intensive
self-examination and self-justification which was to preoccupy modern art henceforth.[20] The question as to the origins of the schism
between art and reality remains untouched, except for one instance
where the philosophical background is briefly introduced,[21] and
Fichte's position is mentioned as the necessary prerequisite to sym-
bolist theory.[22] The author goes on to say that an acquaintance with
Novalis' philosophical endeavors is required for fully understanding
his poetic work,[23] but no investigation of the poet's actual preoccupation with Fichtean thought follows. The rest of the chapter
indicates that both Mallarmé and Novalis thought in terms of
'poetizing the world' (p. 116). However, the concept is treated
mostly from Mallarmé's perspective. Vordtriede's most valuable
presentation establishes Novalis' connection with French Symbolism, but in doing so the author comes to circumscribe the particular

[18]   "Was also in Deutschland seit dem *Tasso* und seit Novalis' analytischen
Bestimmungen in Grillparzers *Sappho*, E. T. A. Hoffmanns *Ritter Gluck*,
bei Brentano, der sich vor der lebenssicheren Alten im *Kasperl und Annerl*
so sehr schämt, einer jener unnützen Dichter zu sein, dass er sich für einen
'Schreiber' ausgibt, zum eigentlichen Thema vieler Dichtungen wird, das
Dichtersein selbst, sieht man in Frankreich nun bei Alfred de Vigny in den
Vordergrund treten" (p. 24).
[19]   "Wenn Opitz im Jahre 1624 sein *Buch von der deutschen Poeterey*
schreibt, muss er zunächst einmal versuchen, der Gestalt des Dichters wieder
einige Achtung zu erringen" (p. 8).
[20]   "Seit Goethes Tasso war der Dichter selbst Gegenstand dichterischer
Darstellung und Analyse geworden. Der Dichter wird allmählich zum 'poeti-
schen Nihilisten'. Am Beispiel Grillparzers kann man diese deutsche Entwicklung aufzeigen und an die Schwelle gelangen, an der Vigny steht" (p. 13).
[21]   Vordtriede, chap. vii, pp. 112-122.
[22]   "Erst seit Fichte ist es möglich, das Objekt als Symbol des Subjekts zu
behandeln. Indem das Ich sich selbst als Weltschöpfer entdeckt, wird es sich
zugleich dessen bewusst, was ihm als Nicht-Ich, als Objekt, entgegensteht.
Und das, was es nun in neuer Erkenntnis begreift, kann es nur symbolisch
wiedergeben" (p. 113).
[23]   "Novalis' philosophische Position scheint Solger im einzelnen nicht ge-
kannt zu haben. Mit ihr aber muss man sich beschäftigen, will man die
theoretische Notwendigkeit erkennen, die ihn zur Erschaffung der Symbol-
sprache drängte" (p. 115).

question to which an investigation of the "Fichte Studies" would furnish an answer.

It cannot be our task to substantiate or disprove a thesis as far reaching in historical scope as is the concept of the artist's increasing estrangement from reality. The "Fichte Studies", limited as they are to one poet's philosophical speculations over the span of two years, would hardly prove to be conclusive evidence. Nonetheless, these philosophical fragments show in minute detail the intellectual processes which transform the concepts of moral philosophy into those of an all-pervading aesthetic dynamism, and only after aesthetics have been elevated in this manner can the alienation mentioned by Vordtriede take place. An agreement between our findings and the more inclusive theories concerning the artist's position in modern times is of mutual benefit: the true significance of the "Fichte Studies" in their historical context becomes more apparent on the one hand, and, on the other, the complexity of the concept of art's estrangement from reality becomes more lucid from the perspective of one of the beginning stages in the process of alienation. The previous chapters have shown as decisive a difference between Fichte's philosophy and Novalis' interpretation of it as exists between ethics and aesthetics. Let us examine the difference between ethics and aesthetics once more in order to see whether it might not lead to a better understanding of the artist's final estrangement from reality, and, conversely, also to a better understanding of the "Fichte Studies" themselves.

Kant as well as Fichte uses the novel approach of Critical Philosophy to preserve very traditional ethical values; inadvertently they also preserve an equally traditional severity against the physically founded self which has always accompanied such values. Even though the ethical standards are old, the method used for insuring their validity is new to such a degree that it involves a complete reversal of the traditional relationship between subject and object. The subject is seen in a determinative role where previously it was considered to be passive. In words that have since gained almost proverbial currency, Kant illustrates the new dynamism with which the subject has been endowed by comparing his revolution in the conceptual realm of philosophy to the one wrought by Copernicus in the physical realm of astronomy:

Es ist hiemit ebenso als mit den ersten Gedanken des KOPERNIKUS bewandt, der, nachdem es mit der Erklärung der Himmelsbewegungen nicht gut fortwollte, wenn er annahm, das ganze Sternheer drehe sich um den Zuschauer, versuchte, ob es nicht besser gelingen möchte, wenn er den Zuschauer sich drehen und dagegen die Sterne in Ruhe liess (Vol. III, p. 18).

Kant accomplishes his revolution according to the principle "that we perceive of objectivity a priori only what we put into it ourselves" ("dass wir nämlich von den Dingen nur das a priori erkennen, was wir selbst in sie legen", p. 19). The concept of objectivity per se is not subject to this law until Fichte proclaims the absolute unity of subject and object in the prime act of self-positing (*Tathandlung*). Kant separates the given unity of 'appearances' (*Erscheinungen*) into their subjective and objective moments not in order to proclaim the subject's autonomy, but rather to set its theoretical powers a limit in the 'thing in itself'. He limits the realm of speculative reason in order to furnish the negative foundation for the metaphysical principles of practical reason, or, as he himself states it: "Ich musste also das Wissen aufheben, um zum Glauben Platz zu bekommen" (Vol. III, p. 25). The *Wissenschaftslehre* is nothing else but the attempt to furnish the positive formulation for the metaphysical principles of that very same practical reason. Fichte's motive is the same as Kant's, since he also wishes to establish the law of ethics on an absolute foundation which will withstand all the onslaughts of doubt generated by human reason. Both philosophers, regardless of their differences as to how far positive formulations of absolute values may be carried, agree completely in their common insistence on the absolute nature of ethical standards of free action. For Kant as well as for Fichte, ethical action is free self-enactment, that is to say, it is the self-manifestation of the idea of man in an empirical instance. In an ethical act, man is simultaneously free agent, material, and product: free agent, because he acts according to the dictates of his absolute nature; material, because it is his physical existence which is formed according to the idea of humanity; and product, because the resultant fusion of freedom and physical dependency constitutes that empirical phenomenon which in contrast to all others may be defined as a human being. Kant and Fichte envision man in the process of creating himself out of the clay of physical objectivity by means of the free act of ethical action. An ethical man is the empirical image of the absolute idea of man, he is the only product of man's only action, he is, in effect, THE 'made thing' (*poiema*), THE work of art.

The moralism of Kant and Fichte inadvertently leads to that unique fusion of ethics and aesthetics which, if translated into the terms of art, is nothing else but the fundamental position of German Classicism. From the aesthetic standpoint the disharmonious strife between the absolutely founded 'ought to' of the ethical imperative and the demands of physical existence which ultimately are doomed to submission is most unsightly. The artist, therefore, seeks out that point of unity, that point of harmonious tangency, which must underlie all relationship, even that of opposition. Schiller's theories on aesthetics are one untiring attempt to balance the forces of moral duty and empirical inclination within art's harmonious sphere of beauty. Schiller knows that his is an aesthetic demand which may claim man as its object only to a limited degree; beyond those limits the demands of ethics must reign exclusively: "Überhaupt gilt hier das Gesetz, dass der Mensch alles mit Anmuth thun müsse, was er innerhalb seiner Menschheit verrichten kann, und alles mit Würde, welches zu verrichten er über seine Menschheit hinaus gehen muss."[24] The full realization of the harmony Schiller envisions is possible only in the realm of art, the realm where the seriousness of man's standing embattled with himself as agent and object is re-solved into play as soon as he chooses an object other than his own self for his formative drive.[25] According to the dictates of ethics, man must be prepared to give up his physical existence, a sacrifice which entails the total subordination of the physical sphere to the demands of the spiritual one. A harmonious reciprocity between those two spheres requires that each retain its autonomy in a unity based on coordination rather than subordination. For Schiller, in his capacity as author of the *Aesthetic Letters,* the point of co-ordination is a point of neutrality. At this point, man is no longer determined by the forces of his physical environment, nor has he yet started to exercise his formative powers as the free agent he is

---

[24] *Über Anmuth und Würde,* Vol. XX, p. 298.
[25] C.f., chap. ii, section C for the relevant discussion of the 'play-impulse' (*Spieltrieb*).

ethically. Within the realm we call the reality of human existence, such perfect neutrality is merely a point of transition which must necessarily be traversed before an ethical act becomes possible. Permanence of the state of neutral balance can be achieved only in the playful unreality of art where the reciprocity of the dualism which is man is unmarred by opposition. The words in which Schiller defines the harmony of aesthetic play have already been cited, but for the purpose of clarifying the present argument, they must be reemphasized once more:

Der sinnliche Trieb will bestimmt werden, er will sein Objekt empfangen; der Formtrieb will selbst bestimmen, er will sein Objekt hervorbringen: der Spieltrieb wird also bestrebt seyn, so zu empfangen, wie er Selbst hervorgebracht hätte, und so hervorzubringen, wie der Sinn zu empfangen trachtet (Vol. XX, p. 354).

Despite the proximity of ethics to aesthetics in Schiller's speculations, a complete merger of one with the other does not take place. The two realms, although intimately related, remain separate. In the realm of empirical reality, the ethical imperative must rule supreme as the chisel which fashions the image out of the processes of physical existence. The medium for ethical enactment is the empirical human being who, in his capacity as medium, constitutes the point of tangential unity at which the demands of duty and inclination, of spirit and body, meet. In the realm of art, that very unity which is man stands depicted as harmony, as the perfectly coordinated reciprocity between the artist's formative power and its object.

As Edgar Lohner has pointed out in his recent work,[26] Schiller has the tendency to replace empirical reality with 'aesthetic illusion' (*Schein*) as the realm of the ideal where man's powers function in the true freedom of harmony. The poet is, however, unable to free himself entirely of the claims made by the moralist. In the essay *Of Grace and Dignity (Über Anmuth und Würde),* it is dignity which has the last word, and the *Aesthetic Letters,* Schiller's most pronounced declaration of the superiority of aesthetic harmony over ethical monarchy, are written as an educational guide towards correct public conduct in the political state.

[26] *Schiller und die moderne Lyrik* (Göttingen, 1964).

The oscillations between aesthetics and ethics, so characteristic of Schiller's writings, are no longer found with Novalis. The gap which Schiller had started to open between aesthetics and ethics, between aesthetic illusion (*Schein*) and empirical reality (*Wirklichkeit*), was closed once more, ironically enough only in order to make the final separation of art from reality possible in modern times. In the previous chapters, Novalis' conceptualization of the basis for all of reality was outlined. It proved to be self-representative action according to a definite schema of representative interrelations, so that the harmony Schiller envisions in the realm of aesthetics, exclusively, comes to permeate all existence as its fundamental law. For Novalis, ethics, as the law of empirical human existence, and aesthetics, as the law of harmonious unity, have merged completely in his concept of all-pervasive representative action. For Kant and Fichte, the categorical imperative of absolute ethical standards was the guide for human self-realization; for Novalis, it is the law of absolute harmony which is man's foundation, guide and fulfillment. Novalis' position is by no means one which simply declares the superiority of artistic endeavors over other aspects of human existence. As familiar as such a hierarchical categorization might be to the present-day reader, Novalis is a stranger to it. The "Fichte Studies" show no hierarchy in that sense; they merely establish that principle which Schiller had incorporated in his concept of play-instinct (*Spieltrieb*) as the principle of all action whether it be absolute or empirical. The fusion Novalis effects between the principles of aesthetics and those of Fichtean ethics is unique.

If we reexamine our findings in their historical context, then Novalis, the thinker and poet, appears to have reached the final stage of a pivotal process in the history of ideas. The theories of Kant and Fichte are prerequisite moments which, as was outlined above, lead to the absolutizing of ethics, and from there toward the possibility of equally absolutizing aesthetics, a possibility realized initially by Schiller and conclusively by Novalis. The famed *kalokagathia* of German Classicism actually constitutes that fleeting point of balance at which aesthetics had come into its own as an equal partner of ethics, only in order to outdistance the latter and to assume absolute authority immediately thereafter.

The attempt has been made in these pages to trace Novalis' initial steps in a direction which leads away from the divinity of ethics, in whose honor Fichte had still erected his edifice of thought, toward a potentially equal glorification of the aesthetic. Novalis' reinterpretation of Fichtean philosophy during the years of 1795 and 1796 must be viewed as the final step which was to usher in the new era of art's isolated supremacy.

BIBLIOGRAPHY

This bibliography is limited to those works which either are mentioned in the text or have had a direct influence on the ideas expressed in this book.

Albrecht, Luitgard, *Der magische Idealismus in Novalis' Märchentheorie und Märchendichtung* (Hamburg, Hansischer Gildenverlag, 1948).

Allemann, Beda, *Ironie und Dichtung* (Pfullingen, Günther Neske, 1956).

Barth Karl, *Die protestantische Theologie im 19. Jahrhundert: Ihre Vorgeschichte und ihre Geschichte* (Zürich, Evangelischer Verlag A.G., 1947).

Benjamin, Walter. *Schriften*, Edited by Th. W. Adorno, Vol. II, 420-528 (Frankfurt, Suhrkamp Verlag, 1955).

Bollnow, Otto Friedrich, *Unruhe und Geborgenheit: im Weltbild neuerer Dichter* (Stuttgart, Kohlhammer Verlag, 1953).

Bonarius, Gerhard, *Zum magischen Idealismus bei Keats und Novalis* (Giessen, W. Schmitz Verlag, 1950).

Bracken, Ernst von, *Meister Eckhart und Fichte* (Würzburg, K. Triltsch Verlag, 1943).

Carlsson, Anni, *Die Fragmente des Novalis* (Basel, Verlag Helbing Lichtenhahn, 1939).

Carlyle, Thomas, "Novalis", *Critical and Miscellaneous Essays.* Edited by H. D. Traill, Centenary Edition (London, Chapman and Hall Ltd., 1899), Vol. XXVII, 1-55.

Cassirer, Ernst, *Philosophie der symbolischen Formen,* 3 vols. (Berlin, Bruno Cassirer Verlag, 1923, 1925, 1929).

Dilthey, Wilhelm, *Das Erlebnis und die Dichtung* (2d ed., Leipzig, B. G. Teubner, 1907).

The Works of Dionysius the Areopagite, (Now First Translated into English from the Original Greek), Translated by John Parker (London, James Parker and Co., 1897).

Drechsler, Julius, *Fichtes Lehre vom Bild* (Stuttgart, Kohlhammer Verlag, 1955).

Dyck, Martin, *Novalis and Mathematics.* ("University of North Carolina Studies in the German Languages and Literatures", No. 27.) (Chapel Hill, University of North Carolina Press, 1960).

Eisler, Dr. Rudolph, *Kant-Lexikon* (2d ed., Hildesheim, Georg Olms Verlagsbuchhandlung, 1961).

Feilchenfeld, Walter, *Der Einfluss Jacob Böhmes auf Novalis.* ("Germanische Studien", Heft 22.) (Berlin, Verlag von Emil Ebering, 1922).

Feng, Tscheng-Dsche, "Die Analogie von Natur und Geist als Stilprinzip in Novalis' Dichtung" (Dissertation, Heidelberg, 1935).

Fichte, Johann Gottlieb. *Sämmtliche Werke,* Edited by I. H. Fichte, 11 vols. (Berlin, Verlag von Veit und Comp., 1845-1846).

Fischer, Kuno, *Fichte's Leben, Werke und Lehre.* ("Geschichte der neuern Philosophie", Vol. VI, 4th ed.) (Heidelberg, Carl Winter's Universitätsbuchhandlung, 1914).

——, *Schiller als Philosoph,* 2d ed. (Heidelberg, Carl Winter's Universitätsbuchhandlung, 1891).

Fridell, Egon, *Novalis als Philosoph* (München, Bruckmann, 1904).

Fuchs, Emil, *Vom Werden dreier Denker: Was wollten Fichte, Schelling und Schleiermacher in den ersten Perioden ihrer Entwicklung?* (Tübingen, Verlag von J. C. B. Mohr, 1904).

Geissler, Ewald, *Das empirische Ich oder die Menschen in der Fichtischen Philosophie* (Leipzig, Buchdruckerei Robert Noske, 1904).

Gelpcke, Ernst, *Fichte und die Gedankenwelt des Sturm und Drang* (Leipzig, Verlag von Felix Meiner, 1928).

Goedecke, Karl, *Grundriss zur Geschichte der deutschen Dichtung: Aus den Quellen,* Vol. VI; (2d ed., Leipzig: Verlag von L. Ehlermann, 1898).

Haering, Theodor, *Novalis als Philosoph* (Stuttgart, Kohlhammer Verlag, 1954).

Hamburger, Käte, "Novalis und die Mathematik; eine Studie zur Erkenntnistheorie der Romantik", *Romantik-Forschungen. Deutsche Vierteljahrsschrift für Literaturwissenschaft und Geistesgeschichte,* Buchreihe, XVI (Halle, Max Niemeyer, 1929), 113-184.

Hardenberg, Friedrich von. Eine Nachlese aus den Quellen des Familienarchivs, Edited by "a member of the family" [Sophie von Hardenberg] (Gotha, Friedrich Andreas Perthes, 1873).

Hartmann, Nicolai, *Die Philosophie des deutschen Idealismus* (2d ed., Berlin, Walter de Gruyter and Co., 1960).

Havenstein, Eduard, *Friedrich von Hardenbergs ästhetische Anschauungen. Verbunden mit einer Chronologie seiner Fragmente* ("Palaestra", LXXXIV) (Berlin, Mayer and Müller, 1909).

Haym, Rudolf, *Die Romantische Schule. Ein Beitrag zur Geschichte des deutschen Geistes,* Edited by Oskar Walzel (3rd ed., Berlin, Weidmannsche Buchhandlung, 1914).

Haywood, Bruce, *Novalis: The Veil of Imagery.* ("Harvard Germanic Studies", I) (Cambridge, Mass., Harvard University Press, 1959).

Hederer, Edgar, *Novalis* (Wien, Amandus Verlag, 1949).

Heilborn, Ernst, *Novalis, der Romantiker* (Berlin, Georg Reimer, 1901).

Heimsoeth, Heinz, *Fichte. Geschichte der Philosophie in Einzeldarstellungen,* Abt. VII ("Die Philosophie der neuesten Zeit I, Band 29") (München, Verlag Ernst Reinhardt, 1923).

Heller, Erich, *The Artist's Journey into the Interior* (New York, Random House, 1965).

——, *The Disinherited Mind* (Cleveland, Meridian Books, 1959).

Hiebel, Friedrich, *Novalis; German Poet, European Thinker, Christian Mystic.* ("University of North Carolina Studies in Germanic Languages and Literatures", No. 10.) (Chapel Hill, University of North Carolina Press, 1954).

——, *Novalis, der Dichter der blauen Blume* (Bern, A. Francke A.G., 1950).

Huch, Ricarda, *Die Romantik*. Vol. I *(Blütezeit der Romantik)* (5th ed., Leipzig, H. Haessel Verlag, 1913).

Jaspers, Karl, *Die grossen Philosophen*, Vol. I (München, R. Piper and Co. Verlag, 1957).

——, *Psychologie der Weltanschauungen* (3rd ed., Berlin, Verlag von Julius Springer, 1925).

Kabitz, W., "Studien zur Entwicklungsgeschichte der Fichte'schen Wissenschaftslehre aus der Kantischen Philosophie" (Dissertation, Berlin, 1901).

Kant, Immanuel. Werke, Edited by Ernst Cassirer, Vols. III, V (Berlin, Bruno Cassirer, 1922, 1923).

Korff, H. A., *Geist der Goethezeit,* 5 vols. (3rd ed., Leipzig, Koehler und Amelang, 1958-1960).

Küpper, Peter, *Die Zeit als Erlebnis des Novalis.* ("Literatur und Leben", hg. von Richard Alewyn, Neue Folge Band 5) (Köln-Graz, Böhlau Verlag, 1959).

Kuhn, Hugo, "Poetische Synthesis oder ein kritischer Versuch über romantische Philosophie und Poesie aus Novalis' Fragmenten", *Zeitschrift für philosophische Forschung,* V, No. 2, 161-178, No. 3, 358-384 (Meisenheim, Weltkulturverlag Anton Hain, 1951).

Langhammer, Franz, "Das Novalisbild im Frankreich des neunzehnten Jahrhunderts" (Dissertation, Northwestern University, 1956).

Lohner, Edgar, *Schiller und die moderne Lyrik.* ("Schriften zur Literatur", edited by Reinhold Grimm) (Göttingen, Sachse and Pohl Verlag, 1964).

Mähl, Hans-Joachim, "Novalis und Plotin: Untersuchungen zu einer neuen Edition und Interpretation des 'Allgemeinen Brouillon' ", *Jahrbuch des Freien Deutschen Hochstifts* (Tübingen, Max Niemeyer Verlag, 1963), 139-250.

——, *Die Idee des goldenen Zeitalters im Werk des Novalis: Studien zur Wesensbestimmung der frühromantischen Utopie und zu ihren ideengeschichtlichen Voraussetzungen* ("Probleme der Dichtung. Studien zur deutschen Literaturgeschichte", Vol. VII) (Heidelberg, Carl Winter Universitätsverlag, 1965).

Maeterlinck, Maurice, *On Emerson and Other Essays,* Translated by Montrose J. Moses (New York, Dodd, Mead and Co., 1916).

Mahnke, Dietrich, *Unendliche Sphäre und Allmittelpunkt. Beiträge zur Genealogie der mathematischen Mystik* (Halle, Max Niemeyer Verlag, 1937).

Malsch, Wilfried, *"Europa" Poetische Rede des Novalis: Deutung der französischen Revolution und Reflexion auf die Poesie in der Geschichte* (Stuttgart, J. B. Metzlersche Verlagsbuchhandlung, 1965).

Minor, Jakob, *Anzeiger für deutsches Altertum und deutsche Literatur,* Vol. XXVIII (Berlin, Weidmannsche Buchhandlung, 1902), 82-122.

Müller-Seidel, Walter, "Probleme neuerer Novalisforschung", *Germanisch-Romanische Monatsschrift,* XXXIV (Heidelberg, Carl Winter's Universitätsbuchhandlung, 1953), 274-292.

Novalis Fragmente. Erste vollständig geordnete Ausgabe, Edited by Ernst Kamnitzer (Dresden, Jess, 1928).

Novalis Schriften, Edited by Ernst Heilborn, 3 vols. (Berlin, Georg Reimer, 1901).

Novalis Schriften, Edited by Paul Kluckhohn and Richard Samuel, 4 vols. (Leipzig, Bibliographisches Institut A.G., 1929).

Novalis Schriften, Edited by Paul Kluckhohn and Richard Samuel, 4 vols. (2d ed., Stuttgart, Kohlhammer Verlag, 1960-).

Novalis Schriften, Edited by J. Minor, 4 vols. (Jena, E. Diederichs, 1907).

Novalis Schriften, Edited by L. Tieck and E. v. Bülow (6th ed., Berlin, Georg Reimer, 1846).

Novalis Schriften, Edited by L. Tieck and F. Schlegel (Berlin, Georg Reimer, 1802 [1805, 1815, 1826, 1837]).

Olshausen, W., "Friedrich von Hardenbergs Beziehungen zur Naturwissenschaft seiner Zeit" (Dissertation, Leipzig, 1905).

Overbeck, Helene, "Die religiöse Weltanschauung des Novalis" (Dissertation, Berlin, 1928).

Preitz, Max (ed.), *Friedrich Schlegel und Novalis: Biographie einer Romantikerfreundschaft in ihren Briefen* (Darmstadt, Hermann Gentner Verlag, 1957).

Samuel, Richard, "Der berufliche Werdegang Friedrich von Hardenbergs", *Romantik-Forschungen. Deutsche Vierteljahresschrift für Literaturwissenschaft und Geistesgeschichte,* Buchreihe, XVI (Halle, Max Niemeyer, 1929), 83-112.

——, "Zur Geschichte des Nachlasses Friedrich von Hardenbergs (Novalis)", *Jahrbuch der deutschen Schillergesellschaft,* II (Stuttgart, Alfred Kröner Verlag, 1958).

Schelling, Fr. W. J. von. Sämtliche Werke, Edited by K. F. A. Schelling, Vols. I-III (Stuttgart, J. G. Cotta Verlag, 1856).

Schiller, J. C. Friedrich (ed.), *Die Horen.* Nos. 1, 2, 6 (Jena, J. G. Cotta, 1795-1797).

Schiller, J. C. Friedrich, *On the Aesthetic Education of Man: In a Series of Letters,* Translated by Reginald Snell (London, Routledge and Kegan Paul Ltd., 1954).

Schiller, J. C. Friedrich (ed.), "Xenien", *Musen-Almanach für das Jahr 1797* (Tübingen, J. G. Cotta, 1797), p. 296.

Schillers Werke, Edited by Julius Petersen, *et al,* Nationalausgabe, Vols. XX-XXI (Weimar, Herman Böhlaus Nachfolger, 1962-1963).

Schlaf, Johannes, *Christus und Sophie* (Wien, Akademischer Verlag, 1906).

Schubart, A. *Novalis' Leben, Dichten und Denken* (Gütersloh, C. Bertelsmann, 1887).

Schulz, Gerhard, "Die Berufslaufbahn Friedrich von Hardenbergs (Novalis)", *Jahrbuch der Deutschen Schillergesellschaft,* VII (Stuttgart, Alfred Kröner Verlag, 1963).

Simon, Heinrich, *Der magische Idealismus. Studien zur Philosophie des Novalis* (Heidelberg, Carl Winter's Universitätsverlag, 1906).

Spring, Powell, *Novalis, Pioneer of the Spirit* (Winter Park, Florida, The Orange Press, Inc., 1946).

Steiner, Rudolf, *Novalis als Verkünder des spirituell zu erfassenden Christentums* (Dornach, Schweiz, 1930).

Striedter, Jury, "Die Fragmente des Novalis als 'Präfigurationen' seiner Dichtung" (Dissertation, Heidelberg, 1953).

Vordtriede, Werner, *Novalis und die französischen Symbolisten* (Stuttgart, Kohlhammer Verlag, 1963).

Walzel, Oskar, *Euphorion. Zeitschrift für Literaturgeschichte,* Vol. IX, Nos. 2 and 3 (Wien, Carl Fromme, 1902), 456-486.

Wellek, René, and Warren, Austin, *Theory of Literature* (2d ed., New York, Harcourt, Brace and Co., 1956).

Wundt, Max, *Johann Gottlieb Fichte* (Stuttgart, Frommanns Verlag, 1927).